Between Heaven and Earth

By FRANZ WERFEL

In this important new book, [...] Werfel, the author of "The Sor[...] Bernadette," "Forty Days of Musa Dagh," and other novels known throughout the civilized world, presents a personal confession which takes on universal significance.

"Wherein Lies Man's True Happiness?," "Ego and Death," "How and What Shall we Read?," "Intellectualism and Success," "Christ and Israel," "Snobs and Sentimentality," "Spiritual Dullness," "Why Faith in God?," "The Issue of Sin," are just some of the topics Franz Werfel discusses in this volume.

In BETWEEN HEAVEN AND EARTH the reader will find a sea of information; thoughts, concepts, and emotions, as clear as the sea, and as deep. This is an inspiring book, a helpful book.

BETWEEN
HEAVEN AND EARTH

FRANZ WERFEL

—

BETWEEN
HEAVEN AND EARTH

Translated by *MAXIM NEWMARK*

PHILOSOPHICAL LIBRARY
New York

First Printing

"The essential, only and profoundest theme of the history of the world and of mankind, to which all others are subordinate, is the conflict between skepticism and faith."

From Goethe's notes to the
"West-Oestlicher Divan."

Foreword

The four chapters of this book are four documents of a lengthy battle. This battle was and is being waged against a certain all-powerful and all-dominating state of mind, designated in the following pages by various names, of which "naturalistic nihilism" is probably the clearest and aptest. I, the author of these polemics, was certainly not born far from the state of mind of naturalistic nihilism, but, so to speak, in its very bosom. As a son of the European liberal middle class, I grew up and was educated in the spirit of humanitarian autonomy and assurance of progress, in the naive nursery faith in world improvement through science, in deeply skeptical negation of metaphysical, religious, not to speak of mystical thinking and feeling, and in the most fatal confounding of liberty with moral anarchy. If it was my good fortune to break away at an early age from this mental atmosphere that surrounded and fostered me, I owe it, first of all, to God, but then also to my love for and inclination to poetry, which taught me from the very beginning to revolt against the empty shallowness of the materialistic-realistic interpretation of the world. To be sure, the process that I have just lightly designated by the words "break away," was far from being a simple and single act, but rather a winding, serpentine path, that all-too-frequently led me back to the same place. This book, therefore, contains not only four documents of a battle, but four stations along this winding, serpentine path, the end of which is just as unknown to me, the traveler, as the day of my own death.

Why are there exactly four documents or four stations? The reason is of purely external nature. As a refugee from two European countries, Austria and France, I have not only lost the majority of my unpublished manuscripts, but also many of my minor publications that appeared between 1910 and 1938 in German, Austrian, and other European periodicals and annuals. In the compilation of this book I was accordingly limited to those of my writings which existed in German in the form of books or pamphlets, and which were available in America. Most important among these are the three essays that compose the first part of the spiritual accounting which I myself regard this book to be: "Realism and Inwardness" (1930), "Can We Live Without Faith in God" (1932), and "Of Man's True Happiness" (1937).

The fourth section, "Theologoumena," which composes the entire second half of my book, was written in America in the years 1942 to 1944, and is now being published for the first time.

The first three parts named above were not written as essays or tracts but were written and delivered as lectures. They were later prepared and amplified, but not altered, for publication. I mention this fact only to explain the oratorical, entreating tone which the reader might find strange if the various titles led him to expect cool, abstract treatises.

It must further be added that I toured the large and small cities of Germany with the first two of these lectures at a time when National Socialism was still struggling for power and when world destiny still seemed to be hanging indecisively in the balance. In half-conscious quixotism I regarded it as my duty to speak with complete frankness to the German literary and student clubs—who, of course, had made their decision long before—and to tell them that the real crux lay not between Right and Left, but between Above and Below. And so it happened one night in darkest East Prussia's sinister industrial town of Insterburg that the students claimed my conviction that humanity could not live without faith in God and without Christianity to be a Jewish Communist trick. Whereupon, amid the howling and booing of the aforesaid students, at the earnest solicitation of the lecture manager, and under the derisive protection of the police, I was forced to leave the auditorium. The right wing as well as the left equally resented my statement that socialism and nationalism are political *Ersatz*-religions—a definition which at that time was not nearly as hackneyed as it is today.

Meanwhile I have learned that it is not only folly but also presumptuous conceit to attempt to change the direction of the dominant trend of the times. Man is very weak. He who claims to be original succeeds at best in becoming a writing, painting, or composing clown. Everyone of us needs a re-connection, a *"re-ligio"*—in its etymological sense—with an established entity. Most people accept the *Ersatz*-religions which the nihilistic spirit of the times offers them as thoughtlessly as they formerly accepted true religion. What hope is there for a daring attempt to move this strong spirit of the times to a feeling of uncertainty in itself, if possible by arguments in its own language?

FOREWORD

Writers are capable of expressing themselves in only two fundamental literary forms—in the form of entertainment and in the form of confession. I trust the reader will forgive me if I offer him the second form in less diluted style than customary.

Franz Werfel

Beverly Hills, California
May, 1944.

CONTENTS

		PAGE
Foreword	....	vii
I	Of Man's True Happiness.......................	13
II	Realism and Inwardness	45
III	Can We Live Without Faith in God?.............	77
IV	Theologoumena	141
	A On the Mystery of Incarnation.............	143
	B On the Sacredness of Property.............	162
	C A Few Words on Sin.......................	178
	D On Seeing God	191
	E On Christ and Israel......................	193
	F Profane Addenda	213

Of Man's True Happiness

I

One evening during a time of great sorrow, when I felt that I could never cease mourning the loss of one dear to me, I chanced into the resplendent opera house of an Italian city. They were playing *Mignon* which, as you know, achieved its modest and unassuming immortality despite the hostility of connoisseurs, the scorn of critics, and the disdainful noses of snobs. I expected very little from this particular performance of an opera I had not heard since the days of my youth. What was there to expect? Some insipid amusement to help kill the time, relieved at best by the singular, animated complacency so typical of Italian opera audiences.

"To kill time," what a profound and terrifying expression! Vaguely uneasy in the presence of what is really worth while, we amuse ourselves, we "kill" the brief time of our lives by playing cards, going to tedious moving pictures and plays, or plunging into the meaningless whirl of society.

However, the evening of which I am speaking turned out quite contrary to my expectations. Why, I cannot say. Was it the Goethean cast of characters, that shone indomitably through the veil of the libretto? Was it the plastic grace and nostalgia of melodies learned in childhood? Was it the incomparable heroine? The insipid

13

amusement I had expected changed from scene to scene, more and more intensely, into that pure state of happiness that we shall consider and interpret here, the happiness of art.

When I left the theater that night and walked home through the empty, echoing streets of the foreign city, I asked myself, "What is it? What power dissolved the incessant thoughts of grief in my consciousness and diverted them into spheres of solace?" An old, somewhat musty opera, certainly not one of the great masterpieces of operatic music. Costumed singers, all of whom, with the exception of the title heroine, never as much as troubled to transmit human emotions but merely emitted pretty sounds, circumspectly and with deliberate effect. And yet I had become another person. Projected through the indifferent medium of *Mignon,* pure happiness consoled and exalted me, the delivering grace of tears, perhaps the most unselfish friends of our life.

Instead of finding an answer to my question, on my way home I suddenly beheld in my mind's eye "The Valley of Kings." During a trip to Egypt many years ago I had visited this great, lonely burial place of the Pharoahs in the desert. The Valley of Kings is a well-concealed, bowl-like depression in the hills outside of Thebes, the City of Temples. Insurmountable cliffs in yellow, brown, cobalt-blue and violet hues make this place a colorfully desolate end of the world. In the summery heat of the Egyptian winter you must climb a steep flight of stepping stones half way up the enclosing hills before reaching the entrance to this world of the royal dead. Suddenly you find yourself in a cool, narrow gallery after having walked along a seemingly endless path of rickety boards leading into the hill's interior. Now and then the bright searchlight carried by the Arab guide casts its sharp beam into side vaults and abysses. The unwrapped mummy of some Ramses regards the intrusive visitor with the emaciated but well-preserved visage of an ironically starved intellectual. Soon the path leads into a suite of moderately-sized rooms and chambers which resembles a city apartment denuded of its furnishings. The guide's searchlight illuminates the walls, and behold! they are covered from ceiling to floor with paintings which, after three or four thousand years, have not yet lost their radiant power. In interminable sequence long bands of pictures full of epic vividness are arrayed one beneath the other. They portray the journey of the Sun God through the Underworld, the demonic forces that assail him, the struggles in which he prevails over them, the Court of Souls in the great Judgment Hall where animal-shaped Judges are assembled, and where the good and evil deeds of the departed are laid upon golden scales. In addition to this predominantly religious portrayal, there is still enough room in the burial chambers for the thousandfold scenes of earthly life. All these pictures in the interior of the hill, in the depths of death and darkness, radiate comfort and joy. You see charming minstrel-maidens floating along in dance rhythm, the eleven-stringed psalter or the long-necked lute in their hands, or the double-flute at their lips. A company of soldiers, home from the campaign, stands in martial array. Women and children, who have come out to welcome them, wave with upraised arms. Nubians are threshing grain in rhythmic motion. Other slaves are

15

plucking geese, ducks, and quail. Noble gentlemen are hunting in the marshes; from their slender boats the intrepid heroes slay the lumbering hippopotamus. Meanwhile their wives are entertaining at elaborate receptions. The mistress of the house is introducing her youngest little daughter to her friends. The child is naked so that the ladies can admire her lovely body with suitable exclamations of delight.

These images and many more forced themselves on me with remarkable vividness after I had left the theater. I also saw before me the varicolored columns of the Temples of Karnak and Luxor, those mightiest columns in the world with their lotus-blossom capitals. I saw the long friezes, sculptured in relief, which one can read as an open book. I saw the statues of gods, and of kings at whose giant knees nestled the delicate figures of queens. Under the spell of these Egyptian memories, I was compelled to stop. Were not all these glorious images gathered around the grave's edge only, were they not all turning their shining faces only towards death? Then it became clear to me: Art is the opposite of "killing time." It is the "arresting of time." It is the "killing of death."

Anyone who has suffered the loss of someone close to him, knows how affecting it is to encounter some object which belonged to or was used by the deceased. Things continue to exist after our flesh and blood have turned to dust. The less life a thing has the longer it lives. Stones existed before Man and they will continue to exist when he is gone. But Man went forth and breathed life into the stones. He did it to deliver himself from mortality. He mixed the fiery colors and covered with paintings the burial vaults of his kings in the interior of hills. These vaults were then sealed for all time and secured by mazes of labyrinthine passages against grave robbers and desecrators. The pictures of a beautiful life on the walls were destined to be surrounded with profoundest darkness to the end of all days. And yet the departed would be delighted and pleased by them, by all these perpetuated moments of everyday life, by the dancing maidens playing their instruments, the soldiers, the grain threshers, by the noble huntsmen and the elaborate receptions. Egyptian painting and sculpture are perhaps the greatest of all time because they focused their entire energy upon the thought of death, and by so doing, destroyed that thought entirely. Thus does it lay bare for us a vital root of the arts within the economy of the human soul.

It has remained for our times to neglect the arts as those aspects of life generally printed in small type in the publications. Politics, Technology, Sports, the Stock Market, Business, such are the serious realities that claim the so-called "whole man" even if they quarter him alive every minute of the day. All else is considered mere trimming, "relaxation" after the day's work. The man who has no time all day long is the very man who wants to kill time in the evening. How terrified we would be if ever we stood face to face with the hollow travail of our days. Unlike the ancient Egyptians, we do not know how to master the consciousness of death by moulding it creatively. Modern man lives in a state of constant despair unknown to the ancients. We suffer from the uninspired, even stifled happiness within us. For all happiness is an awareness of the non-existence of death, is a wondrous and joyous realization that there is no death. It is the role of art, and always has been, to imbue us at certain moments with this happiness of the non-existence of death.

How does it happen then that these moments are becoming more and more rare, that people are less and less amenable to creatively liberating rapture?

II

Childhood is the period of genius among the different ages of man. As a child, even the most mediocre individual is compelled to repeat that incomprehensible creative performance which initiates the process of becoming a human being, that of giving names to things, and thereby recreating them. From the avowals of many great men we know that for them the experiences of childhood were the constant impulse to their productivity. Under a cooling crust the hidden magma of their earlier days glowed in them forever as the memory of a fiery-fluid state of the awaking soul.

"What is true of the parts, is true of the whole." This ancient proposition is equally applicable to Man. Our modern intellectual constitution consoles us for the disquieting element of certain primeval truths, neutralizing them by the word myth. Because we no longer understand the disquieting language of myths, we think ourselves obliged to see in them fabulous fantasies and childish tales. Yet is it not remarkable that in the childhood memories of human civilization we find everywhere recorded the story of the Flood and, preceding it, the story of a happier state of the world, the legend of Paradise, or of *aurea aetes,* the Golden Age? Plato speaks of an "ancient people better than we and dwelling closer to the gods." This people, he tells us, were not so far removed as we from the original cosmos, the world of "ideas," which we share only as a faded memory. Church theology also teaches the concept of an "original revelation" which mystically dawned upon the human race long before Sinai and Golgotha.

There are no logical grounds for summarily confining the assumption of a Golden Age to the realm of legend. On the contrary, it can be demonstrated that an original happier state of the human soul on earth is not inconceivable. But before we can do that, we must depart somewhat from the traditional conception and habit of thought which has been impressed upon recent generations. By that I mean the biological conception of evolution. We are accustomed to thinking of the evolution of life as being more or less regulated by a cosmic timetable which indicates, in a fairly punctual way, the stations leading from lower to higher and from simple to differentiated forms. It would be an unbroken line which runs from inorganic matter directly into the organic, from the plant kingdom into the animal kingdom, and finally from animal into man. Only with difficulty can we moderns rid ourselves of this popular, Darwinistic conception, in spite of the fact that not a single investigator has succeeded in throwing any light into the creative abyss which yawns between inorganic and organic matter. To be sure, there are carnivorous, animal-like plants; but creation's flash of genius, which unites these two kingdoms of nature, does not illuminate our minds.

We observe the anthropoid ape, we compare his anatomy with that of the Neanderthal Man, but to what avail? All scientific quests resolve themselves into vague hypotheses because we no longer hear God's pronouncement which raised a quadruped, horizontal creature to an upright position; yes, *raised,* in the splendid dual sense of the word, in the sense of "vertical" and in the sense of "exalted." Nature, with her sphinx-like smile, allows us a premonition of certain interrelationships, but she veils in mystery the conclusive proof of their transition, the only thing that matters. And shall we say that there is no meaning and no conscious intention behind all this?

The same popular, scientific way of thinking also colors our relationship to the so-called primitive peoples, to certain South Sea Islanders, Patagonians, Pygmies, and others. In these both inwardly and outwardly poverty-stricken peoples with their absurd gods, their pitiful explanation of nature, their totems and taboos, we see the state of our own ancestors, a terminal station in the cosmic timetable that is valid for us, too. But even this notion has nothing to support it. Is it not just as probable that these primitive people are a degenerate and ungifted progeny cast off by previous civilizations? Modern science is not averse to considering this question seriously.

Our technological arrogance goes so far that we judge the status of the several epochs of civilization only according to the respective type and perfection of their tools. Whenever I read of discoveries from the Stone or Bronze Age, I am appalled at the shortness of the interval that separates us from our forefathers, who must have been primitive people according to our modern conception. In middle European latitudes, this interval is scarcely three thousand years. So close behind us then, according to the overwhelmingly accepted view, is the time when we were miserable, ignorant, superstitious savages. Is it any wonder that the average man of today, insofar as such thoughts occur to him at all, looks down with shuddering condescension from the height of his modern comfort upon the prehistoric world, and even upon the world of classical antiquity? He considers as rank nonsense the notion that his "progress" might also be a "regress" and that his undeniable rise may have come about at the cost of incalculable spiritual impoverishment. Your average contemporary can scarcely be dissuaded from considering himself an out and out parvenu stemming from the prehistoric cultural void, from the primitive jungle. That he might be descended from the "effulgence and rapture" of the soul, from Plato's ancient people dwelling closer to the gods, seems to him, at best, a crazy dream. Of course, he believes in a Golden Age, to a certain degree. But his political philosophies, each in its respective way, relegate it to the future. He forgets that his historical memory reaches back scarcely more than six thousand years, although, if paleontology is to be credited, his species has been living on earth for thousands of centuries. Is it not extremely naive to think that this short, illuminated stretch of time constitutes all of the history of civilization, while the immense reaches of preceding time knew the erect, walking biped only as a gregarious semi-animal? Who knows, perhaps our race, in the silent thousands of centuries, has risen to and fallen from heights which today cannot even be imagined.

Modern man is loth to accept the truth that certain

creative forces in him are bankrupt, that this great loss has left him a shivering beggar in spite of his strenuously built-up outer physique. On the contrary, he believes himself to be the possessor of a promissory note on happiness which one day will be redeemed when his political *Ersatz*-religion will have created the material prerequisites for it.

What is it, then, that might persuade us not to share these average views of the present-day world? To find an answer to this question, I must begin with another personal experience. Some time ago the subject matter of a lengthy work I had in progress required a rather extensive study of Babylonian civilization. Although this highly-renowned civilization, like the Egyptian, reaches back to the dark boundaries of prehistoric time, it too is only an heir. On the magic soil of Mesopotamia, it had already been preceded by older civilizations, the Sumerian and Akkadian, and before these, by even more obscure ones which only now are being unearthed. In the works that I perused, the intellectual world of old Chaldea emerged as a purely cosmic, or rather, as an astrocentric, symbolic structure. The Babylonian and his cultural predecessors were a people of the stars, in a way now scarcely conceivable to us. The universe of the night sky was the realm into which they projected their earthly life and from which they received in return their transcendental life, in constant interchange. These ancient civilizations are rightfully called the inventors of astronomy, but that does not express the complete truth. Certainly, the Chaldeans developed a scientific astronomy of magnificent proportions. They were the creators of the calendar. They divided the amorphous progression of days into weeks, months, years, and beyond that, into definite aeons or world-years. On thousands of clay fragments which have come down to us, they inscribed the most complex calculations, foretold eclipses of the sun for centuries ahead, defined the orbits of the major planets, predicted the return of comets, described the slow progression of constellations in the firmament. Yet, magnificent as all this may be, it is only a slight part of their essential achievement.

At the present time a strong wave of interest in astrology is again sweeping through the world. Not only a few sensitive Souls are occupying themselves with this study devoted to the fatalistic connection between star and man. Even politicians and stock market speculators consult it before undertaking a *Putsch* or concluding a major transaction. I know barbers and waiters who read horoscopes on the side. Clever astrologers advertise in the newspapers, and less clever ones set up their necromancers' booths with the sign of the zodiac at carnivals and fairs. Everyone knows that the art of horoscope reading as practiced today is not based on personal experiences of our time but has been taken over part and parcel from antiquity. The modern astrologer plies his art like a machine with which, to be sure, he obtains results, but whose structure and mechanics he does not understand. He has learned from the Chaldeans, for example, that Saturn exerts negative influences and troubles the constellations. He counts on this fact but he doesn't know why. Nothing within him sheds light on the mystery. Saturn is nothing to him but an empty name on a chart. Most probably he has never actually distinguished Saturn from the other planets in the night sky. In short, the original spiritual powers have been extinguished in us, and without these powers there can be no essential and vital view of cosmic relationships. The ancient Babylonians, however, and the preceding waves of humanity who were their masters, Plato's ancient people among them perhaps, still possessed these spiritual powers so inconceivable to us, and by virtue of them, performed the stupendous task of deciphering the illimitable cryptograph of the stars in the Eastern sky. And only by means of these powers were they able to discover the high astrological doctrine of correspondences which can be summed up in the Chaldean axiom, "All that is above is also here below."

And now we come at last, after all these apparently devious ways, to the point that I wanted to reach. If we turn our gaze towards the childhood of mankind, as we know it, towards ancient civilizations, it becomes clear that though we have grown incomparably richer in analtic methodology, we have grown incomparably poorer in integrated conceptual power. Realizing this, the acceptance of an *aurea aetes,* of Plato's people close to the gods, of the existence of a glorious prenoachidic race before the time of Noah, no longer seems absurd.

Recently, a natural scientist coined an apt expression for ancient man, saying that he was "nature-sighted." However, I should like to change this expression into "spirit-sighted." For it was more than a natural vision, it was an unexampled spiritual vision by means of which that priestly man of old, with the creative perception of his entire being—all that is above is also here below—divined the negative, depressing powers of Saturn and associated with it such things as lead, dark colors, and the hemlock herb. We must pause a moment in awe at these men and people. Wherever and whenever they may have lived tens of thousands of years ago, on the legendary continents of Atlantis and Lemuria, or on Mesopotamian soil, they performed the most prodigious spiritual feat of our species; they saw the reality of the gods in the phases of the planets, they interpreted them and, assuredly, they also saw God himself. Perhaps they had not yet invented the wheel, nor the ship; perhaps they had only recently evolved the roofed dwelling. Their daily life was presumably far more precarious and exposed than that of primitive man. Yet at night they lifted their clairvoyant eyes and their even more clairvoyant souls to the heavens, and combined the stars into a startling panorama of constellations, and gave each its name. With inconceivable subtlety of mind they arranged the firmament and the chaotic points of light which cover it into the twelve fixed "houses," and made the signs of the zodiac masters of these houses, giving each sign a name. Even today we still say "Leo, the lion," and "Taurus, the bull," "Aquarius, the water-carrier," and "Pisces, the fishes," "Scorpio, the scorpion," and "Aries, the ram." We call the signs of the zodiac by their old names. The professional astrologer knows the influence hidden behind these signs as carried down from time immemorial. But the real significance of the names has been lost to us, as has the living experience of the powers concealed within them. We continue to babble them in good faith. But the very fact that these terms have come down to us, though in an infinitely diluted meaning, provides indisputable proof that tens of thousands of years ago there must have existed races dwelling close to God and tremendously superior to us in cosmic insight and spiritual power of conception.

The Golden Age described in the myths of mankind possessed not only the divine gift of vision but also the no less divine gift of naming things. One need not be an etymologist nor a philosopher of language to be awed by the wisdom and unfathomable significance of human speech. In the beginning was the Word; and the Word was with God; and not until the Word was bestowed upon Man did he become the true child of God. But alas, they upon whom it was first bestowed in all its splendor and fullness after an epoch of stammering attempts, (and by this act God completed the process of "raising Man") —they took the greatest secret of mankind into the grave with them.

"Every word," said Emerson, "was once a poem; now it is a tomb of the muses." Emerson's observation is not merely a beautiful aphorism; its truth can actually be demonstrated. Let us analyze any word, for example, the word "existence." Literally translated, "existence" means "issued-forth-ness" or "set-forth-ness"; and its verbal component is less significant than the prefix "ex," which denotes direction. Thus, the simple word "existence," which we use without thinking, expresses not only the fact of "being" but at the same time confesses that there is no autonomous being, and that all existence has issued forth from something greater. I am therefore firmly convinced that when true human speech was finally evolved out of panting, animal sounds it began not as communicative prose but as rapturous, intuitive song, as spontaneous chant and esoteric incantation. Before factual communication there was poetry.

The luminous figure of the Golden Age is Orpheus. By giving them names for the first time, he enchanted rocks and trees so that they tore themselves loose and followed him. Thus we see Clairvoyance and Poesy standing as the oldest guardians at the entrance portals to humanity. We are indebted to them for all that is good, for they have helped us across the steep threshold. When we forget them we shrink into mere God-forsaken intellects. It is no fairy-tale illusion that ancient myths called the Golden Age the age of happiness, that age ruled by deepest insight and the power of naming things. For what is happiness other than the grace of being permitted to unfold to their fullest bloom all the spiritual powers planted within us?

III

The unimaginable spiritual powers which we are evoking, the original power of insight and the original power of naming things, were at first bound up into one, and so were the objects to which they were applied. Whether planet or zodiac, whether rock or spring, whether tree or animal, all things lived behind the awesome, sacred veil of the numenal, of the divine. In the primordial age of the world there was no cleavage in Man's wholeness of view. Men dwellt closer to the gods; that is, they became aware of the secret meanings of creatures and things by the very fact of seeing them with clairvoyant eyes and naming them with inspired names. The bull, to mention an example, was something quite different from what it is to us. It was more than a mammal with cleft hoofs and horns. The still unspent spiritual powers of Man recognized in it a certain divine quality which, in all creation, was reflected only in the bull. An inconceivably subtle sense divined the sun in the bull and the bull in the sun. Animals not only *were* but they *signified,* even beyond their being. Ancient man lived and thought only in metaphors. And in this we differ from him most profoundly. For to us, things only *are,* but they do not *signify.*

The essential temper of the Golden Age is not documented by any concrete discovery, nor can it be. However, we must necessarily infer its character from those ancient religions and arts that are known to us.

In the post-mythical age, which we shall call the early classical, we already behold the dissolution of that original unity which once had been intoxicated with the morning dew of human creation. The decay of spiritual powers had already begun. Mankind took its first step towards our own epoch. The highly lauded documents that we possess are already harbingers of the first decline. Man no longer sees the gods and the realities mirrored in them. He is no longer the namer of names and of the relationships which these names reveal. His waning, original power begins to separate into various directions, and the first secularization of the divine appears. The mighty trunk divides into three branches: an all-encompassing, pure religion now becomes theology; the intuitive wholeness of view gradually tapers down to investigative science; and the volcanic power of the first giving of names becomes conscious poetry. This process can be clearly demonstrated in extant works. An early epic such as the Babylonian "Gilgamesh," for example, is almost inaccessible to us; we cannot understand it. The reason is that behind the deeds and sorrows of the hero, as well as of his gods, are concealed dozens of cosmic and astral meanings which becloud the narrated action and, like an abstruse thicket of words, confuse the reader who has no spiritual key to them.

Now Homer is quite different. In him everything is "universally human" and "harmonious." Every college student of the classics understands Homer once he has penetrated the armored guard of the aorist and the irregular verbs. This is so because in the "Iliad" and the "Odyssey," which date from about the eleventh century before Christ, those secret meanings are already submerged and secularized. Probably in Homer's day, too, the spiritual key had already been lost for a long time. The orbits of the stars in the night sky were no longer a vital experience; they were merely traditionally accepted. The gods in these epics were already anthropomorphic to a high degree. Whereas in the "Gilgamesh," the gods still completely retain their supernatural character, the man of the "Iliad" has already naturalized his gods and sees them in his own image. When Homer depicts the Oxen of the Sun God, of Hyperion riding the heavens in his chariot, it is a poetic and realistic portrayal, nothing more. The oxen have here completely lost their noumenal significance which had still been alive in ancient Egypt and Babylonia. Yet, we must remember that this very act of personifying the divine at the same time gave birth to classical poetry.

My general theme can also be illustrated by the development of written symbols, from hieroglyphics to the alphabet of letters. In the beginning we find here, too, not the primitive but the complex; that is, hieratic picture writing, a votive system of pictorial symbols by which all things and concepts are expressed in accordance with their religious significance. With the passing of the ages, this hieratic writing of priests degenerated to a demotic, profane style of writing, finally thinning out to our present alphabet which merely links one sound to another. Remains of the original inspiration are still left even in our meager alphabet. But today, how many of us know when we write the letters A and B that the pointed alpha is the triangular symbol of divine unity, or that the circularly closed beta, Hebrew *Beth,* is the profane word for "house," and the metaphysical symbol for the universe?

In the history of mankind there is no progression that is not at the same time a regression, and no regression that is not at the same time a progression. Such is the law of the conservation of historical energy. The Fall of Man, the banishment from Paradise, the forfeiture of original happiness,—whatever we may choose to call the mystery of the vanished unity of our original spiritual powers,—we must not only attribute to it all our life's sorrow; we are also indebted to it for infinite advancement. True, the trunk was divided into several branches; but the luscious fruit does not grow upon the trunk; it grows upon the leafy branches. In the Golden Age there was, to be sure, intimate living with the gods, but no religion; there was a prophetic outburst of song and story, but no organized art of poetry and music. Before these could be, it was necessary for the flaming sword of the Angel to flash and the thunderous pronouncement of exile to sound out. Only then could a suddenly-blinded Man begin his journey out of degradation and through the stony wastes of history, to that goal of salvation towards which he blindly aspires. Not wholly naked was he when the sentence of exile sent him forth. Though he lost his spiritual vision, yet the spirit accompanied him in various guises. The consciousness of God remained with him; so did art and the faculty of speculation. Of these, it is art with which we are primarily concerned, for art is the most merciful reflection of the ancient powers of the soul in exile, wandering in the diaspora of modern life. Each time that almost incommunicable ecstasy touches us at the experience of some work of art, the sundered spiritual powers of the Golden Age are once more brought together in us for an instant.

In the words above I have ventured a definition. Every true poem has the power of evoking in a susceptible reader a long lost state of singular delight. In this re-awakening lies the deepest secret of esthetic effect. The Aristotelian theory of "pity and terror" is already a restrictive explanation. For it is not the subject of a work of art that arouses artistic excitement within you. If it were anything material, something translated out of life, then how could pure music exert an effect? Indeed, you find it impossible to express what it is in an original melody that affects you so wonderfully. You only know that your whole being tenses and expands, your self-esteem grows and your baser ego, with its petty, insignificant thoughts, becomes completely submerged. The consciousness of death recedes into nothingness; a

31

comforting certainty of never dying sets your entire being aglow for one timeless, flashing instant. The original melody has given back for a few seconds what had been taken from you at the gates of paradise. With the hymnal response of your soul you give names to things for the first time, you grow aware of relationships, you come closer to the divine. The recollection of an ancient state of happiness has touched you.

Plato was constantly dealing with recollection in this sense. As the spiritual power of *re*-cognition, it is a ruling idea of his system. Only by "recollecting" a spiritual cosmos in which we too once lived, are we in a position to recognize "ideas," that is, to know them once again.

Plato's idea of recollection also explains the strange emotions which we owe to art. In a life of attrition our soul suddenly recollects its innate powers; it becomes temporarily "spirit-sighted" and returns to itself in its original wholeness. In a strict sense, the intuitive spirituality aroused in us by a picture, a song, or a thought, is the one and only quality—Plato calls it *mania*—which transports us into a state of pure happiness. All other pleasures belong to the baser order of the satisfaction of instinctive urges.

IV

We realize now that the arts are not recent discoveries in the cultural rise of mankind. On the contrary, they were the prime requisites, the great apriori of this rise. We realize, too, that the arts are still intensely alive with those original, impalpable, spiritual powers which have been gradually sacrificed to civilization. In the plastic

arts the human soul's assurance of immortality perpetu-
ates the fleeting vision by giving it form. In the literary
arts the Word, echoing forth from an impassioned heart,
casts its spell not only on that which it describes but also
on its metaphysical meanings.

The history of the arts, like all that is human, is not
a record of linear progression but a general advance in
ever-renewed cycles and spirals. In contemplating these
cycles we constantly see the same law revealed. From
its groping beginnings, art each time climbs with favored
swiftness to its highest level, steadfastly religious and
symbolic. From that point on there is a decline to the
bitter end of a given epoch characterized by an equally
steadfast realism and naturalism. This is no less true
of the history of Egyptian and Greek art, with all its
spirals, than it is of medieval mural and panel painting,
which finally degenerates into a non-functional, autonomous easel-painting. Over and over again, on a minor
scale, we behold the same act of secularization, the same
withdrawal of mankind from the divine. But not for its
own pleasure does the world become untrue to its Creator. It is a superhuman compulsion that each time forces
it down, a process of weariness and atrophy, strangely
mingled with the bitterest defiance. In the age of myth,
the first Adam, the newly created and exalted image of
God, however primitive his life may have been, nevertheless saw supernatural meanings everywhere in Nature.
And what is realism in contrast to this? It is the defiant
will to insignificance, to meaninglessness. The realist
with his enfeebled soul fears and denies the mystery
created in things although it had been the first and foremost meaning of all art to sing of this mystery.

With the word realism, however, I come to our own age which we must somehow try to understand. I shall not commit the romantic error of one-sidedly condemning a world in which we are obliged to live and, indeed, in which we desire to live. We are the victims of our age, no matter whether we see the cause of our sorrow in material and political deficiencies or in metaphysical decay. To understand a phenomenon, however, we must not only see it clearly but we must also judge it fairly.

The comparison of the ancient world with childhood, the period of genius among the ages of Man, suggested itself quite naturally. In the concept of childhood is hidden an infinite capacity for learning, extravagant giving and taking, naive acceptance, passionate belief in one's own permanence, eternal living in the moment, lack of consistency and lack of the burrowing will to ferret out the meaning of things. In such colors do we see the portrait of ancient man. In this portrait, however, we also see reflected the transfigured pallor of another period of life. It is the noble countenance of an extreme old age reminiscent of those hoary, venerable figures of classical antiquity.

To which age of humanity shall we now compare ourselves? Before deciding, let us consult the average "philosophy" of our day.

Our contemporary does not believe in his heart that creation is a spiritual phenomenon and that, consequently, its meaning and goal must also be spiritual. He entertains certain confused notions of a materialistic economic origin and goal of humanity. His most cherished dream is a justly regulated order of society which assures everyone a full measure of earthly welfare. Out of this welfare the final miracle of civilization will blossom forth like a golden age. It is amazing how much the political ideologies of the day, for all their mutual animosity, resemble each other in this one anti-metaphysical point. Whether based on nationalism or internationalism, on biology or economics, they differ only slightly in this naive belief in the future, this profoundest disbelief which constitutes general materialism.

Now, at which time of life do we think the most in economic and materialistic terms? Certainly not during childhood, nor during the time of our youth which is too much under the domination of the instincts. Man begins to think in terms of economics when his passions have abated and Eros no longer threatens him with catastrophes. The post-climacteric man past fifty might serve as an allegory of the economic and materialistic age. We see him as the symbol of a pinchpenny, a skinflint who has been cheated of everything, and who stumbles through the streets of the city, mad with despair. He had believed in nothing but material securities, particularly of the interest-bearing kind; and it was this very belief in security and securities that had been mortally struck by fate. Such, too, was the belief of Harpagon, the aging miser, who symbolizes the materialistic age. And Harpagon's ruling obsession was that spiritual phenomena are only the superstructure of social and economic conditions.

However, such fanciful comparisons can be carried to extremes. The portrait of the aging skinflint is crossed by that of a grimly determined youth who goes through misery gritting his teeth and clenching his fists. And yet, our age, which we here portray in allegories, is vaster than the most enlightened of our contemporaries might suspect. For here, too, that inexorable law of balance holds true; namely, that every gain signifies a loss, and every loss a gain. We were first compelled to renounce the spirit in order really to conquer matter. We first had to lose the transcendental world in order to win this world. The only question is whether the prize of our victory is living or dead.

The conquest of this world at the cost of the transcendental world! In all the millenia that passed between the age of the first wagon wheel and about the year 1830, the technological relation of man to his earthly environment did not essentially change. The accomplishment of the Phoenicians who, at King Solomon's behest, sailed around the Cape of Good Hope to reach Ophir was not one whit less great than the nautical accomplishment of Columbus, and subsequent feats of discovery. Throughout this period of time the extent of the earth's surface, the unconquerable vastness of space and the isolation of the various cultures remained about equal. Not until the middle of the last century did that tellurian revolution begin whose breath-taking force only the most callous could underestimate. The vastness of the earth's surface melted, space was conquered, and isolation gave way. Truly, it is not to be wondered at that contemporary man began to believe that no one like him had ever lived before. He no longer merely dreamed of the bright sky overhead; he actually rose up into the stratosphere to see what was there. And behold, there was nothing! For Man is only capable of discovering what he himself carries with him. We can spare ourselves the tedious enumeration of all those immortal feats which have finally led to the construction of hundreds of bomber squadrons and to the assiduous penetration of the ether by jazz music, political speeches, boxing bouts, international sports and amateur hours.

Across the portrait of our allegorical Harpagon moves another face. We see the features of Prometheus, seamed by lightning. If ever a time has earned the name of Promethean, it is ours. But Prometheus is chained to the rock and Zeus' sharp-beaked vulture is tearing out his liver in revenge for his betrayal of metaphysics, that is, the theft of the divine fire. The liver and gall were, according to the ancients, the seat of melancholy and of life's despair. And our age, too, the true age of Prometheus, suffers from life's despair. In illustration of this I shall not point to the dreadful chronicle of suicides in our newspapers but, paradoxical as it may seem, to pictures of apparent joy in living: I see gaily-pennanted, sun-swept bathing beaches before me. They are densely strewn with rabid bathers, men, women, and children, an orgy of exuberant human flesh. The crowd is so great, and the space so limited, that through the packed throng of bodies scarcely a speck of sand can be seen. I see a troop of panting, knapsack-laden tourists, their climbing gear belted to their packs. Theirs are not the bright, carefree faces of strollers. Theirs are the tense, grim, determined features of record breakers. Tomorrow they intend to take some northern or eastern mountainside by assault. Adolescents among them furiously exert themselves far beyond their capacity. These summer and winter pictures of our modern frenzy for nature, sports, and travel can be multiplied at will a hundred-fold. To observant eyes they reveal something deliberate and forced, very far removed from the expression of genuine pleasure.

These triumphs of speed and of exceeding one's physical capacities resemble a willful drunkenness induced by cheap intoxicants. They are a kind of gregarious, week-end narcosis eloquent of the inner emptiness of a type of person who cannot be alone. What does it all mean? What have we lost that we are so grimly trying to regain? Why do we fling ourselves at nature with such passionate vulgarity, like desperate pariahs? We can no longer bear her stillness. Our awe of her has disappeared. The very ones who claim to be neo-pagans desecrate a hypocritically deified nature by their mass rowdyism, just as they dishonor mankind by their politics.

The facial traits of our time betray a dismal, cold-snouted worship of everything sordid. From Germany resounds a convulsive cry in glorification of suffering and death. Now, to be sure, suffering and dying are possible without any special gift; but joy and the capacity for happiness do require a most definite talent.

We need not emphasize the fact that in our half-Harpagonian and half-Promethean age the prevailing tendency in art is a realism devoid of meaning. In dictator-ruled countries it is even officially prescribed, and every deviation from it leads to excommunication and ostracism. In these countries it bears such resounding names as "Heroic Optimism." What does this mean? Let the artistic creator beware of giving things any other meaning except the obvious and generally acknowledged one, that is to say, no meaning at all. And especially let him beware of uttering even a single breath of despair at the meaninglessness of what he is creating. This is a stagger-

38

ing innovation. The dictators actually demand a religious acquiescence to the misery of the people who are blessed with them. So great is this misery that entire nations have been stupefied to such an extent that they are no longer conscious of it; and many people in countries which are still untouched are burning with the fanatic desire to be mastered likewise, and to be morally emasculated. For, to submit to the strong and to emasculate the weak, not only morally, has been the one and only heroic deed of this neo-heroic outlook.

Any admission of despair at this emptiness is punished with the most terrible censure as "subversive." But the only true value of this realism lies in the fact that it actually is subversive in that it confesses its own misery. As a result, this "optimism" commanded and subsidized by the State destroys every possibility of higher intellectual and artistic achievement. Dictatorially governed states decline into a cultural *rigor mortis*. The actual scene before us confirms this conclusion in dreadful measure. We need only recall the photographic paintings of nudes and the colored picture postcards which the smug representatives of "heroism" contrast with a "degenerate" art, doubtless to the shuddering horror of posterity.

Lest there be misunderstanding, let me explain that in this concept of "realism," I am not opposing the faithful portrayal of reality in favor of some diluted symbolism. The world is spread out before the artist and poet exactly as it is, in all of its merciless clarity, so that they can shape it and give it meaning. He who approaches the world with faded similes and borrowed metaphors is a jaded epigon or dilettante. The true artist and poet exalts what he sees in reality into a *vision*. No matter how acute an insight may be, nor how faithful a reproduction, nor how impressive a portrayal; though it may even arouse our admiration for its author's gift of observation, it is still far from being a poetic vision. The perfect statement of a fact, the fashioned material itself, evokes no meaning. It is only the *vision* of a fact which unveils its meaning and lets us divine it. Herein lies the great difference. A merely realistic book broadens our knowledge of the ponderable. An inspired poem opens our eyes to the imponderable. True art is a kind of atomic disintegration of matter, caused by primordial spiritual powers which persist more vitally in the artist than in other men.

The common notion that there are no longer any true artists in our day must be emphatically denied. There are as many of them as at any other period of history. They share, in a singular way, modern Man's general hopelessness. Though there always has been only a limited circle of initiates who are innately true artists, today they are forced, as never before, to live in catacombs. The gulf between the creator and his audience is growing wider from year to year. Which of the two is to blame? In those arts involving handicraft, such as painting and music, the unwholesome isolation is especially pronounced. A sense of detachment and incompatibility forces the finest talents into extreme esotericism, since they do not wish to become degraded purveyors to a pleasure-seeking clientele. Twenty-five connoisseurs create for twenty-five connoisseurs. Huddled together in mutual hostility, the little group finds itself suspended in a vacuum.

However, we should not ignore the fact that even radical art has won some pyrrhic victories. The ornamental swamp flowers and creepers of the secessionists moved into middle class living rooms at about the turn of the century, just as today the walls of many a cafe are softly painted with cubistic and futuristic monstrosities without anyone's taking offense. Even the wildest cacophonies of modern composers have already been domesticated into incidental music for gangster films.

Unfortunately, however, even this esotericism of art for art's sake is only an estimable error. For esotericism that does not point to the supersensual is no esotericism at all. The modern art of our radical artists falls into an error similar to that of the all-engulfing common realism. For realism considers only the material; radical modern art is concerned only with the means of expression. Again a clear symbol of decay!

We must, of course, not forget that the creative spirits of today are confronted with an almost unsolvable problem. The tyranny of the times compels them to abnegate those ancient powers of the soul through whose possession alone they are creative spirits. What adamant assurance is needed to disregard the taboo which is laid upon such ambiguous concepts as "pathos," "romanticism," "mysticism"! How tempting it is to throw off the frightening loneliness of a hopeless struggle and to align oneself meekly with one of those philosophies which offers to its blissful adherents not only life but also a higher irresponsibility.

And yet, only the rarest nonconformists, only those eternally lonely and independent spirits will ever reconsecrate our desecrated world by interpreting it and themselves.

V

Two lines of verse are ever in my mind. They are from the following lovely poem by Lenau:

HEAVENLY SORROW

Across the face of Heaven glides a thought,
A dark, foreboding cloud infused with woe;
Like to a man who sleeps with soul distraught
A windswept branch is tossing to and fro.

A melancholy moaning fills the Sky.
Behind her lashes lightning soon appears.
So eyes will glisten when about to cry,
And through the lashes tremble shining tears.

Now from the marshes steal the cooling rain
And gentle fog across the heather-land;
And Heaven, dreaming of her vanished pain,
Slowly lets the sun drop from her hand.

If you let these splendid lines re-echo in your mind, you will certainly understand why it was this poem in particular that occurred to me. Its innate power illuminates and confirms the train of ideas that we have been following. Lenau's "Heavenly Sorrow" is a marvelous example of how, even in latter days, those original powers of the soul suddenly open their eyes and make themselves manifest. Consider the first two lines of the opening stanza:

Across the face of Heaven glides a thought,
A dark, foreboding cloud infused with woe.

42

The grave, majestic march of the first line, the dragging cadence of the second, why do they move and delight us? A simple picture, the evening sky and a lonely, moving cloud, nothing more. A simple metaphor, heaven and face, cloud and thought, nothing more. And yet, by the figurative comparison of two comprehensible quantities a third incomprehensible quantity is made perceptible. An inexpressibly profound and penetrating insight into an existence that reveals itself only to metaphor is disclosed to our perception. The "spirit-sightedness" of a poet arouses our own long-buried "spirit-sightedness." We suddenly begin to see and hear with senses that have not yet been dulled by the custom of thousands of years. What we see and hear in that brief moment of esthetic emotion strengthens our soul with mysterious sustenance and, exulting, it desires to bestow on others the happiness it has received. I have quoted two lines by Lenau, but anyone can probably cite verses by other poets which stir the soul as much. And through a hundred metaphors in which comprehensibles are matched, the ray of the incomprehensible will touch us again and again.

How rich we are in spite of all! What an immeasurable heritage we possess that continues to grow in secret despite all suffering and decay! In art, music, and poetry gleams the indestructible treasure of a grace that forever gives and demands no sacrifice. In every inspiration of art and music there is intertwined a ray of the first revelation. That is why such inspiration brings happiness. For a few moments it leads us in entrancement back to our origin, when our still unified spiritual powers, envisioning things and giving them names in joyous rapture, first became aware of the divine.

We must guard against thinking that the powers and treasures of the muses are an empty adornment which has nothing to do with "practical" life. Only those unfortunates who have never been touched by them try to convince us of that. There is no political problem of humanity that can dispense with these spiritual powers. Peace, the reconciliation of nations, and the struggle for Man's dignity, all have their deepest roots in them. The neo-barbaric fanaticism of masses nurtured on hate can only be destroyed by the luminous inspiration of those eternal powers that stood at the cradle of man's creation. Every victory that is not blessed by them will be a defeat, a deadly, disillusioning variation of the same old misery. For they alone make for permanence; they alone are mankind's only great destroyer of death.

The Creator made Man an upright being, but the long journey through history bows him down again and again. We who are so mighty that we fly through space and harness the waves of the ether are at the same time staggering along the road weary unto death, with downcast eyes fixed on the ground. Is it so hard to raise our heads? Does not the consuming passion for something higher still burn inextinguishably within us? Our soul has never lost Plato's recollection of *mania,* of the ecstatic state of our early dawn. Our alienation and the materialistic delusion of this present will dissolve like a horrible dream. And among the benevolent forces tenderly waiting to wake man out of this dream stand the prophesy and poetry of art.

Realism And Inwardness

It was something of a task to devise a title for this essay that would be adequately indicative of its contents. It deals with problems of art, but not, I hasten to remark, with esthetic questions connected with music, painting, drama, or the novel, or with the psychology of the artist. It is a bit difficult after an earthquake to converse about the architecture of the houses that have collapsed. This essay, then, deals with the full, vital scope of art. Its title might be amplified to read: "The Inwardness o Man and the Fatal Peril That Threatens It."

It is a hackneyed truism, frequently expressed in editorials, lectures, and conversation that we are living in an age of radical realism. Many writers gifted with enviable clairvoyance have tested and analyzed this fact, as generally acknowledged as it is trite, and have conjured up new prophetic vistas out of its implications. They have shown us the ideological pincers that threaten to put an end to our outmoded culture. They have properly named the jaws of these pincers: Capitalism and Communism.

The cardinal principle of Marxist dogma is this: Man, as an individual or social being, is the product of economic forces. What the pre-scientific world called "soul" is only the psychological superstructure of these forces. The inner life of Man is completely predetermined, a waste product, so to speak, of economic chemistry. And the official soviet eschatology teaches that "a classless social order" will produce a stabilization of spiritual life, when human society has once conquered the anarchic physical forces, including, of course, those of economics.

Capitalism, on the other hand, has no official dogma, but gets along very well with the doctrine of Behaviorism. This strangely repulsive word designates a school of psychological thought and is adequately symbolic of the capitalistic state of mind. While Sigmund Freud, as a true heir of Schopenhauer and Wagner, recognizes two demonic forces, Death and Love, that hold tragic sway over the inner man, Doctor Watson, the inventor of the curious little word "Behaviorism," regards the inner man simply as a jumping jack. This mediocre marionette obeys the strings of functions and reactions, and any fool can pull these pedagogical strings to produce the desired results.

In Behaviorism as well as in the communist ideology we perceive a collectivist longing for standardized human manufacture. Everyone wears the same hat and the same opinion. And the capitalist or communist conviction to-day permeates all lands and all classes of our modern world of radical realism, no matter whether they adhere to it openly or whether they regard themselves as the most obdurate reactionaries.

It is with deliberate intention that I use the word "realism" rather than "materialism"; for, unless it is loosely used in a banal sense, materialism is logically only a narrower sub-concept of realism. The word realism has a long and somewhat varied history. It played a role in the late medieval controversy between scholastics and humanists. At that time it was adopted by the orthodox group in distinction to the nominalists who promulgated Aristotelian doctrines. It appeared again at the beginning of the nineteenth century as a technical term in literature and art. In the struggle against the stylized, symbolic and idealizing tendencies of the classical and romantic movements realism was rediscovered. We owe to it the age of Balzac, Flaubert, Zola, Maupassant, Dostoyevski, Tolstoi, Manet and their successors.

But apart from its historical determinants, what does realism mean in its broadest, cultural sense? Clearly, it is man's direct attitude toward the things of life, his most unbiased relationship to nature, unclouded by religious, political or other abstractions. And that brings us to the decisive point: does the radical realism of our age correspond to this valid definition? Is it really man's new-born, sincere attitude toward nature, his unbiased relationship to all the things of life, his conquest of all abstractions?

Before answering this question, we must pause a moment to reflect. If life is a shoreless stream, then the total consciousness of mankind is tossing upon it like a tiny leaf, flung forward and back, whisked right and left, but for the most part, whirled around in circles. Since memory is too infinitely brief to follow these erratic movements, and furthermore, since there is no shore to serve as an orientation point, even the most enlightened atom of this consciousness can formulate assertions about all possible things but not about the direction of its course. And thereby concepts like progress, evolution, and development are, in a cognitive sense, completely ruled out. Modern research is beginning to suspect that the planet Earth has already absorbed many vast aeons of culture, in comparison to which so-called historical mankind represents but an inconsiderable fragment. That is why there is always an aura of artificiality and speculative dalliance about modern philosophies of culture and theories about the "Rise and Decline of the West."

In only a single respect has the radical realism of latter decades lived up to its program. It has made man aware of his physical self in a hitherto inconceivable way. One can very well speak of man's discovery or, indeed, of his conquest of the human body. I am thinking not only of health fads, sports, outdoor life, the seashore craze and women's clothes, but of an even far more intensive growing intimacy of man with his physical self to an extent that has not yet made its effects historically visible. This major achievement of modern realism has, as we shall soon see, an uncommonly symbolic significance. Nature abhors a vacuum; that is why man's famished spirituality pounces on the object closest at hand, on the body. It is a withdrawal from a world completely shorn of reality, to the only pasture, so to speak, that still affords some nourishment. The modern cult of the body, of the adored flesh, is the contrary of what our contemporary prophets foretell; it is, to use a scrambled figure, the last shirt that radical realism has left to the human soul.

Is it paradoxical to say that realism has shorn the world of reality? By no means! Indeed, the assertion can be amply corroborated. History scarcely knows a more unreal, a more abstract age than the present one which considers itself fairly bursting with reality. Let us take technology as an example.

A walking tour is the realest way of becoming acquainted with a portion of the world. But a railway journey deprives the route of reality; and a trip by airplane dissolves the ground over which we fly into a two-dimensional, cinematic, black-and-white impression. One might almost formulate this into a law: reality varies inversely as the square of the degree of perfection of its technological mastery.

Please do not misunderstand me. I am not making a plea for the stagecoach. Personally, I like nothing better than an automobile ride at a 60-mile-an-hour clip. Sighing for a lost leisureliness is the most cowardly and most abhorrent expression of incurable philistine souls. But technology is our terrible fate; we dare not be conquered by it.

To pursue the argument further, I think we can all agree that the farmer, in the sense of our definition, is the realest type of human being. As a part of nature he changes as little as nature herself. For thousands of years his work has remained the same. However, world industrialization has proletarianized large masses of the farmer class. And now, what does the workingman's reality look like? He stands in a machine-filled workshop and performs the same speed-up manual operation six times a minute, eight hours a day. Could anything be more unreal, more unworthy of a human being, more diabolical? It is not because of the hard labor—the farmer works much harder—but because of the unreality, the abstractness of the work, that a factory is an inferno. That is why, for a just man, there can be no more burning question than that of the workingman.

Modern technology envisages the elimination of the small farmer, the destruction of the original nucleus of society, by means of immeasurably vast, grain-growing combines. Whether this will be of practical value and create improved production, I cannot judge. But one thing is certain, if it succeeds, the last vestige of our kinship with the soil will disappear and the universal nomadization of man will be accomplished.

After even these few examples, we arrive at the conclusion that radical realism is precisely the opposite of what it claims to be, although it theoretically dominates the world in conjunction with its innumerable subordinate disciplines, such as historical materialism, biological determinism, pragmatism, positivism, or economic determinism. However, there is no point in quarreling about words, even when they lie.

For, indeed, the question involved is no mere theory; it is a conviction. Every conviction is an assertion of values. Every assertion of values creates schisms. Every schism produces fanaticism and aggression. The enemy, the object of hatred of the realistic conviction, is man's inwardness, his soul, his creative spirit.

There are two causes for this hatred, an eternal, metaphysical one and a temporal, historical one. The former, the eternal, is the Luciferian, Promethean attempt to make the here and now independent of God; the latter, the temporal, arises out of the inverted sense of inferiority felt by uncultured nations or classes of society which physically conquer those culturally superior to them. The aggressive realistic outlook is always revealed whenever a national or social reversal of strata takes place. When the victorious barbarians entered the refined atmosphere of Rome, they certainly must have quieted their inner plebeian insecurity with their indestructible sense of realism. Though Roman ladies may have had a hundred vials of perfume upon their dressing tables, the Germanic woman back home was still the better housewife. Fernando Cortez counterbalanced the impression of the superiority of Aztec culture by bombarding Mexico with his cannon. And today, the word "intellectual" or "esthetic" is a favorite epithet of scorn on the lips of every boor.

Modern realism as a general outlook was also born in an age which witnessed the reversal of social strata, the age of the French Revolution. A highly intellectualized world went down in the general whirl. Its disappearance, of course, was entirely just. In a lengthy process, the spirit had been gradually severed from its metaphysical, religious roots. In appearance it still continued to dominate society, but it had fatal doubts of its own validity. Such was its course from the Encyclopedists to Kant's theory of knowledge. Skeptic always rhymes with septic; the spirit died of intellectual poisoning. What remained was a slough of cynicism wherein rule was to be taken over by the new man, the *bourgeois*. Whoever wishes to maintain his rule must offer the world some potent and tangible ideal. Faced with this dialectical necessity, the *bourgeois* looked about for a *bourgeois* ideal. Now what did he find in the society that had preceded him? - the two great ideal categories which have existed as long as historical man himself: the heroic ideal of chivalry and the ascetic ideal of religion. The newcomer felt himself incapable of these supreme values. What had he been before? A petty tradesman, a shopkeeper, an accumulator of possessions, despised by the ruling spirit and the prevalent scheme of values, an absolute contrast to the priest or the knight. But one thing he had never known and never understood, and that was leisure, which is the origin of all spirit. He had struggled and slaved day in, day out, restless and full of care. Why? Was life so hard? Not in the least! It was merely empty. To be able to tolerate leisure one must be a veritable capitalist of inwardness. Consider the lazzaroni lolling on a waste-heap, whistling - at least he has music in his soul. But work was the utmost form of unselfishness of which the new ruling class was capable. Thus the *bourgeois* created the ideal of work, which still rules the world to the present day. The morality of achievement became the only way to beatitude.

Of course, it was a startlingly novel ideal. What had always been considered unrefined suddenly became the supreme value. The ideal of work, the new *bourgeois* meaning of life, operated as a tremendous impulse. For the first time in the memory of man an ideal triumphed that did not endanger life, an ideal that even brought a bit of material profit. With magic swiftness the world was transformed. It yielded to the materialistic impulse with greater masochism than it had ever yielded to a spiritual one. Weaving looms and spinning machines were improved, and multiplied with dreamlike speed. Pygmy factories grew into smoke-spouting collossi. The bright and cheerful centers of towns were surrounded by immense suburbs with endless house-fronts, breeding consumption and suicide. It is a story that we all know. The petty tradesman had now become an industrialist, a man of business with care-lined features; and business had become an absolute, self-sufficient, undisputed world-power.

Out of himself alone the petty tradesman would never have been able to bring about this situation. He needed an ally, or rather, a creative slave. And he succeeded, to a considerable degree, in gradually subjugating the spirit to the modern realistic outlook with its ideal of work. Hitherto, the son of a clergyman, teacher, civil employee or *petit bourgeois* had gone to one of the many university towns to study theology, philosophy, and among the more progressive, jurisprudence. Each of these young men, in Germany at any rate, had odes and sonnets, not to mention elegiac couplets, hidden away in his desk. Some of these young men became great poets and philosophers; others became excellent readers and listeners, persons of understanding and feeling. Outwardly they led a threadbare existence, but since opportunity was small and their inner compensation great, they did not suffer. Together they formed the fruitful soil out of which grew the Golden Age of German literature.

In its procession of triumph the realistic outlook dared not permit such talents and powers to be lost to it in fanciful idleness. The so-called new reality asserted its rights. It needed mechanical inventions to lower the cost of production, to economize on wages, to beat competition, to drive down transportation rates and, by a sort of black magic, to create markets out of nothing. The arcana of the new physics and natural science had to be released from their abstract formulae and mustered into practical service. And, as a result, most of our budding Hoelderlins and Hegels locked their desks and their hearts and began to tinker with mechanical contraptions. Power, money, and acclaim beckoned alluringly; for, while the laurel is a noble plant, it is exceeding rare, and, for all its rarity, not very rich in sustenance. The inventor and engineer now joined the manufacturer and

53

promoter, and they were all happy together. For the most sought-after gods of the time bear the names of Captain of Industry and Chief Engineer, names which glitteringly embody the supreme power of the present day.

To repeat: the modern realistic outlook springs psychologically from the inverted feeling of inferiority of a rising caste which possesses no values with which to counter a previous cultural superiority. In order to maintain itself in the face of the heroic and religiously ascetic hierarchy of values, it creates its own ideal inherent in its origin, character, and history: the ideal of work. By work it understands nothing but economic activity, that is, feverish engagement in the production and consumption of goods, in other words, money-making. *Extra pecuniam non est vita.*

This process goes so far that as early as the end of the 17th century (the century that paved the way for this new state of affairs), Richard Baxter of Cambridge, a Puritan tract writer, maintained that of two ways of doing business the more lucrative is also the more Christian. Here, indeed, was a herald of the metaphysics of prosperity! The senseless meaning of "work" is not to satisfy needs but to arouse them. To this end, it debases the results of the exact sciences into technology. But in directing its entire endeavor toward making the unnecessary necessary, the realistic outlook demonstrates its completely unreal character. The most terrible and most conclusive consequence of its fundamental unreality is the proletarianizing of all humanity, that is, the removing of all humanity from reality. And so we have the speed-up system, abstract work, tenement houses, and mass misery.

For the sake of intellectual honesty we must emphasize the fact that an historical condition cannot be explained in terms of only a single causal series. The causes of each individual moment of life are infinite. The parallel development of scholarship divorced from dogma and of a bourgeois class plays a far more complex role than can be described in a few words.

The realistic outlook with its ideal of work was also obliged to develop new virtues to replace with some semblance of dignity the ideals of the pre-bourgeois and pre-industrial world. To heroic courage and religious depth it opposed a strenuous activism and an enthusiastic faith in progress. But the supreme rank among the new virtues was held by "efficiency," which is an art for art's sake virtue, so to speak. For the capitalist world considers the most efficient individual the one who can achieve the paradoxical, who can create goods out of air, and markets out of the sky. Indeed, the realistic outlook with its activism and efficiency are the incendiaries which have set the world afire with mammoth production and market imperialism.

The present scene reveals to our gaze a hitherto undreamed of advance of technology. The unreality of economic life is approaching the boiling point. The vicious cycle of clamorous supply and dwindling demand is a throttling noose around the neck of society. The machine, which began by debasing masses of people into an industrial proletariat, continues, as it nears its perfection, to debase them further, ten times more cruelly, into a proletariat of unemployed. If the Lord permits the splendid wheat to grow in Canada, people elsewhere starve to death. If the coffee crop ripens overabundantly in Brazil, there is a consequent and equally overabundant crop of suicides in New York. It is obviously a very real world, isn't it? Truly, one must be a learned economist at the very least if one is not to be engulfed by its unreality.

In spite of all this, the realistic outlook still holds top listing on the exchange, enjoying the esteem both of the guilty and of the victims. How astounding it is to read in newspapers and biographies obsequious eulogies of, for example, a great manufacturer of automobiles. His workmen may generally be fit for the grave at the age of fifty, but before that they are permitted to clutter up the streets with their own rattletraps, and incidentally to provide an additional market for the factory. Try as I will, I cannot help thinking that if such a manufacturer is a great man, then every petty tradesman, who outstrips all the other petty tradesmen of his neighborhood by some fortunate sales method, is a great man. Between him and the great manufacturer there is no general, essential difference, but only one of level and degree.

Whether one organizes the manufacture and distribution of automobiles, emery paper, or soap, and whatever the technical achievements involved, it is all only a matter of efficiency and commercial farsightedness. This farsightedness may even be of prophetic scope, but since it is always relative only to emery paper, automobiles, soap, or matches, it has, to be sure, a good deal to do with utility but nothing with creative greatness.

This is precisely the essence of our problem. What the realistic outlook despite its extreme efforts had failed to accomplish in the entire course of the 19th century, it achieved almost effortlessly in the single decade following the first World War: the intimidation and suppression of human inwardness and the devaluation of the creative spirit. It deprived our soul of faith, and particularly of faith in the soul itself. A terrible proof of this lies in the fact that youth and revolution, once the constant defenders of life against death, are this time standing not on the side of the victimized but on that of the victimizers. In the light of this realization, communism appears as the natural-born, legitimate son of capitalism. Though still an unruly child, it is showing its family traits more and more clearly every day. Instead of a great number of entrepreneurs, the Russian State is the one and only pan-capitalist. No longer does it exploit a single class of wage slaves; this time the entire people, without exception, consists of wage slaves. Total proletarization has led to total removal from reality. The State, now an arch-capitalist, makes use of its absolute power by unscrupulously abolishing the right to strike, the fight for higher wages, and the freedom to form associations. For these it substitutes the narcotic of its adulterated ideology, sustained not by its false, statistical logic but by the stale pathos of long-vanished, heroic days of revolution.

"Happiness *is* virtue, not its reward." If you invert this profound thought of Spinoza, you understand why the world is so miserable today. Man's false ideals are his unhappiness. The false ideals of nationalism have led to death's bargain counter of war, and the false ideal of economic determinism has led to the miseries of capitalism and communism. Blasphemy always carries its own hell within it. What people call reality is and always has been only a fraction compounded of life and of the prevailing outlook. If the outlook is perverted, the result can only be an age of ill feeling.

At this point I should like to postulate an axiom: *without inwardness there can be no external world, and without imagination there can be no reality.*

There is nothing involved about this statement; on the contrary, it expresses a very simple and ancient truth that every one of us experiences personally at every moment. Consider any primitive function, eating, for example. Whereas the lower creatures seek the nutriment most suitable for them and adhere to it, man has developed an infinitely differentiated and discriminating taste. Our sense organs, both tongue and palate, react to hundreds of fine stimuli, whereas the animal apparently must be content with two or three. Thus we experience with every meal a hundredfold reality which simply would not exist if we swallowed food merely as a hunger-appeasing substance full of calories. The differentiation of taste and the discriminating appetite of the human race is a prodigious biological feat, not of our sense organs but of our mind in its struggle for freedom and individuality. By an inward, physical, sentient interpretation of a mouthful of food, we translate it into psychic terms, really *experience* it, that is, we give it a reality which it does not in itself possess.

I have deliberately chosen a homely example from the lower spheres of life to show figuratively that in man's existence there is no reality that is not a child of his creative soul. Man is the measure of all things. But the complex of attitudes that we have termed the realistic outlook reverses this ancient Socratic and Platonic truth and asserts that things are the measure of man. That is the core of all contemporary theories such as economic determinism, environmentalism, historical materialism, and so on. Were it only a matter of animal-like feeding rather than tasting, these theories would be right. But as it is, they effect a reversal of causality, a *hysteron proteron* of the most naive aplomb. Economic determinism asserts that the origin of great historical movements, Christianity for example, can be traced back to the pauperization of the masses in the late-Roman Orient. This arrant nonsense can still be found in Nietzsche's "Slave Revolt of Morality" (*"Sklavenaufstand der Moral"*). If Christianity had been nothing but a doctrine of social ethics, though ever so exalted, we should never know its name today. It was the Christ-impulse alone, the explosive substance of a hitherto unattained differentiation of human inwardness that fundamentally recreated reality.

Things have become the measure of man. That is the key definition of modern technology. Since it is our inescapable fate, we must go through and beyond it. Technology promises us the solution of the problem of life by the complete subjection of cosmic forces to its purposes and by the thoroughly rationalized reconstruction of society. In view of the present situation, we cannot repress our doubt of its therapeutic methods.

Novalis says in one of his loveliest poems:

> *"Help us fetter spirit of earth . . .*
> *And discover life's true worth."*

These two lines are inseparable in their brilliant unity. But the outlook of radical realism divides them; it wants only to fetter the spirit of earth. To "discover life's true worth" is idealistic heresy to realism, a detestable impulse of its arch-enemy, the soul. As the communist eschatology has already shown us, realism's intent is to destroy individual consciousness in order to supplant it with an easily controlled collective consciousness less aware of its misery. And not only in Russia, but everywhere, though in varying degrees, realism is following the same tendency. It is served by a hundred means, from political party discipline to the field of sports. An immeasurable imbecility is arising. The "standardized" brain is triumphing. We are threatened by a regimentation of life and outlook in contrast to which the old Prussian barracks was an innocent county fair. The future belongs to the drill sergeant in every sphere, not only to the party drill sergeant but also to the drill sergeant of letters.

What is to be done? Cries of despair, though ever so passionate, are of no avail. We must try to broaden our understanding.

Every ideal that relates to the shaping of humanity's existence, and hence the realistic outlook too, is eudaemonistic and has as its ultimate goal the realization and propagation of happiness. In what way is the eudaemonism of the prevailing belief in material things striving toward this human happiness? - By endeavoring to alleviate the material misery in the life of the masses, and so, finally, to bring about a humanly dignified state of non-suffering. The most valuable political party produced by the belief in material things, European Social Democracy, has earned high recognition in this respect, in spite of its tragic failure at the outbreak of the World War.

Although we recognize, in all justice, that radical realism is to a great extent the hungry dream of a debased humanity, this sad realization must not prevent us from exposing it as a fatal error of logic. The state of non-suffering is indeed a prerequisite of happiness, but it is far from being happiness itself. To comparative comfort must be added something else so that man will not be destroyed by his own barrenness. To return to my previous metaphor of eating: in addition to the mere assimilation of food there must be a discriminating, relishing, experiencing taste. Anyone who has ever lost his sense of taste as the result of a head cold knows that even the satisfaction of a need can become a torture.

What, then, is happiness? I find only one tenable formula: happiness is the wealth of a reality transfused into inwardness. But why seek new formulae when the formula has already been pronounced long ago, a formula whose truth thunders through the ages: "The Kingdom of Heaven is in yourselves!" The realistic outlook digs for the treasure in the wrong place. Its capitalist side, by virtue of its sterile ideal of work, accumulates surplus value, that is, potential happiness, not in order to enjoy it, but in order to let it continue to work for the purpose of new accumulation. How true is the humorous chain of words concerning the parsimonious testator: "The father denies himself so that his son shall deny himself, so that his grandson shall also deny himself . . ., etc." On the other side we hear communism's conception of happiness: perfect material harmony by sacrificing the spiritual individual and his metaphysical conditions. Both forget that human spirituality may be suppressed perhaps for decades, but not forever. Both forget that the Kingdom of Heaven and the chance of salvation lie only within ourselves. Both forget that happiness is spirit. The realistic outlook and the belief in things is a false and, in an all-human sense, heretical ideal, and as such more dangerous than cancer, more contagious than spotted typhus, and more stupefying to the brain than paresis. However, false ideals cannot be shattered by criticism. Right ideals must take up the battle against them. The fateful question of our civilization is whether the spiritual outlook, which still lives in scattered places, is strong enough to oppose the realistic outlook.

The creative inwardness, the intellectual and spiritual man, is revealed in the three spheres of religion and morality, science and speculation, art and imagination. How deeply destruction has already penetrated into these spheres can be estimated only approximately. The decline of formal religion, at any rate, seems to be considerable. The proletariat has adopted in its entirety the liberal atheism of its leaders. With few exceptions, the great masses of workingmen adhere to this threadbare denial of God. So does the average city dweller, at least in the tenor of his life, even though to some extent he retains his religious affiliation.

It is always the same old story. The intellectual fashion of yesterday becomes the mass banality of today and, like second hand goods, sinks to ever lower levels until it is finally sold off at the most obscure odds-and-ends shop. The Catholic Church withstands the assault of anti-metaphysics with resilient strength. The observer sees signs of its revival in certain countries. One is reminded of Lichtenberg's brilliant classification of people who still believe and those who are beginning to believe again. The Church counts both sorts among its adherents. But as long as it is forced to the defensive, the Church may perhaps produce martyrs but no Saint Thomas and no Saint Francis.

It goes without saying that modern science, for the most part, is in the camp of the realistic outlook. If mercantilism was the father of this child, then nihilistic conviction was its mother. Our modern scholarship steadfastly clings to specialization and modestly closes its eyes to the interpretation of the universe and to pure philosophy.

In so far as science evolves a picture of the universe it is atomistic and agnostic, despairing of knowledge. To see any meaning in universal events it considers an illusory, unscientific prejudgment. This word "unscientific" is its great anathema, the sentence of excommunication which it wields more inexorably than the theologians of the Middle Ages. In the analytic methods of science is concealed a perverted delight in showing the universe its meaninglessness. In physics, the supreme discipline of modern times, the tendency toward emptiness of concept and toward the idle game of logic is asserting itself. There is an attempt to desert the language of words and its imagery and to think only in abstract formulae. Causality is denied, wonder of wonders! The outlook of radical realism simply cannot rid itself of the secret, Luciferian unreality that is locked up in its historical beginnings.

We must not forget to mention the universal superstition that conquered our souls at the same time as the victorious realistic outlook: the deification of the intellect. The early realistic, Kantian era, which we have erroneously regarded as idealistic, assumed that the human intellect was the seat of absolute *a priori* facts, the exalted seat of the transcendental categories of space, time, and causality. Our highly realistic epoch, less philosophically minded, still sees in the intellect an absolute force whose task it is to disintegrate all the conditional ties of man, especially our mythical heritages, ties of nationality, race and family, religious, primitive awe, etc. This type of intellect-deification is most radically represented by psychoanalysis and its neighbors. Instead of praying to the Kantian categories, they pray to the "consciousness" as an *a priori* essence full of a magical power of healing.

But all these superstitions were destroyed long ago by modern physics in the following axiom which Einstein formulated, as early as 1905: "Nature is so constituted that it is impossible experimentally to determine absolute motions." If we apply this irrefutable knowledge of cosmic space to spiritual space, we obtain a principle that was already familiar in the most ancient of days: "The spirit is so constituted that it is impossible intellectually and deductively to determine its truths."

There is only one spirit but there are a thousand variegated intellects. So it is in nature; there is one single absolute motion, but there are a thousand relative, moving points of observation that obscure it. This means that man's fixed frame of reference is determined not rationally but esthetically. The individual man is the sentient representative of his physical type of constitution, of his family, of his social and national heritage, and of a hundred other relativities. Mastery over these can grow only out of a quite rare religious and ethical act, but never out of an intellectual decision. For the intellect is the more or less emotional, poisoned weapon of man's esthetic frame of reference against other hostile frames of reference. He who deifies the intellect makes the source of errors the goal of knowledge.

There is still the third sphere, the sphere of the muses. It is here that I am obliged to express my credo: only the man favored by the muses can rebuild the inwardness that has been destroyed by the belief in things.

Mind you now, I do not mean art, nor works of art, nor even the artist. I mean the man who is moved by the soul and spirit, the man of sympathetic emotion, capable of rapture, full of imagination, receptive to the world, infused with sympathy and holy grace, the man who, in the widest sense, is musical. Is it not strange that in the course of history all types of men have had their turn at ruling the world, but not he? No, it is not strange after all, since power and ambition are always associated with the horror of a vacuum. The man of facts, of deeds, the performer, the doer, the maker is almost always empty and rigid, burned out by the will to power.

The curse of polypragmasy that brought about modern mass misery has never been more keenly pointed out than by a great man who stood at the very cradle of the bourgeois era, Blaise Pascal. In his thoughts on "Human Misery" he writes: "The most intolerable punishment for the human soul is to live with itself and think of itself. For that reason the soul is constantly concerned with the effort to forget itself, by occupying itself with all manner of things that prevent introspection. And this is the cause of all tumultuous activity . . ."

The man favored by the muses, on the other hand, is the fulfilled one, the keeper of the keys to that Kingdom of Heaven which lies within us. Contrary to popular belief, such favored characters are not rare in the world. We meet them a hundred times. The man of the muses can be recognized by the way in which he observes some incident on the street, by his absorption in a moving picture, for example, or by the tilt of his head when he listens to music. He appears in all classes and professions, though he is generally unaware of his grace. I go even further: all people have the spirit of the muses at their core. In the majority it has been buried only by care and the realistic outlook. Others again, poisoned by false ideals, deny this spirit within them. Remember the legend of Orpheus whose singing and playing carried away not only the animals and trees but the very stones. The stones signify the most rigid principle of objectivity, but even in them is concealed something Orphean that responds to Orpheus. Somewhere I once read that we are all born musical but that, as a result of certain inhibitions and our education, we become unmusical. That seems reasonable to me, for I myself know young children, by no means child prodigies, who have learned to play the piano by a certain method and who recognize difficult intervals and analyze sustained chords without looking at the keys. And no special gift nor absolute pitch is needed for this. Of course, I am speaking of music only as a part for the whole.

Imagine what it would mean if the latent music slumbering within us all could be awakened. Anyone who has even once had some profound musical experience, knows that those who have never had such experiences are beggars. We, who with steadfast conviction fight against the misery in the outer world, why do we abide so much

misery in the inner world? The realistic outlook quite
naturally shrugs its shoulders with indifference. It considers all this far more unreal than a game of bridge,
for example. But I ask, what an immense increase of
happiness on earth there would be if every human could
have the nourishment of melody? And music is only a
single sphere. What undiscovered worlds still slumber
in the eye's power of experience, what delights in the
universe of speech, what an intensification of existence
in the heavenly ascension of thought? But we can expect
no such awakenings, we who are faced with war. And
the guilt will lie with the spiritual ignominy of the political and economic leadership of the world. For all that
is evil and stupid on earth is not a superhuman, fateful
inevitability; it is a deadly form of unimaginativeness
and unmusicalness.

Life is a phenomenon of consciousness; and things,
in so far as we actually experience them, are inner es-
sences projected outward. That is why there is no other
happiness than that of love, that of the muses, and, in
its broadest sense, that of the spirit.

Radical realism and technology, however, father and
mother of proletarization and permanent economic catastrophe, must complete the work they have perpetrated.
No one dares stay their hands. The reactionary lamenta-
tion which is still heard, the hollow croaking for vanished
ways of life, for privileges and the like, the hysterical,
rabble-rousing howls for a Third Reich, the potential
horrors of which the healers and howlers themselves
cannot even foretell, all this is only mystically garnished
imbecility and a traffic block.

The realistic outlook cannot be mortally struck in its

material power; it can only be assailed where it is truly vulnerable, in its unreality and inner emptiness. And it is the spiritual ideal embodied in the man of the muses that is called to become the dragon slayer. To be sure, this may seem utopian at first, but it is not at all meant to be. I know that I am announcing revolution, the revolution of life against abstract regimentation.

He who was a revolutionary only once in his life, was never a revolutionary at all. He who is satisfied with having his group come to power and who then crawls safely under the wing of his party or class, is a jaded fellow traveler, not a revolutionary. Revolution is as eternal as the false ideal of power. Its great secret is that its fighting front incessantly changes. Today both the capitalistic and communistic belief in things are arrayed on the side of reaction, lying in the same trench as allies. To discerning eyes their entire difference is but a nuance.

We, however, who wish to defend life, we must assemble, we must mass our forces into a revolutionary irridenta of world friendship against world devastation. This is no utopia! The revolution of the spirit and of the soul comes with the same inexorability as did the materialistic revolution, although in different form. Its final cause will be the vicious economic circle to which I have repeatedly referred.

Even if the realistic outlook should succeed in solving the external problem of existence, it will still go down to destruction. For the very progress of technology and the future lessening of labor are the poles that generate the current of the new revolution. The deeper significance of the machine is that it produces not only goods but also leisure. This leisure, the fatal, splendid surplus value of future man, is the dynamite that one day will blast the first breach in the solid wall of materialism. The superlatively subtle instinct of the communist doctrine of salvation identifies its classless kingdom of heaven with the death of the individual soul. How true this is! A living soul, after four hours of mechanical labor, could never endure ten hours of freedom in the communist or capitalist style, even if it received by way of compensation a hundred thousand bathing parks, football games and boxing bouts, film sensations and miles of automobiles.

However, the social and economic revolution must and will be victorious first of all. That means that individual capitalism will disappear more and more into social capitalism. This process will be accompanied by a period of incalculable poverty. We have just now experienced its beginnings, both materially and spiritually. Cruel as it may sound, in an historical and dialectical sense this state of misery is necessary; for no appeal, no tract, and no sermon will with such impact rouse mankind to the spiritual revolution as will this situation created by the realistic outlook, this secular desolation of the inner life.

Will the coming revolution of the spirit find its promulgators ready? Were we to judge according to the present state of affairs, the answer would be negative. Let us consider briefly the spheres of culture. What is the state of literature? To limit the discussion I shall consider only German literature, and in particular, only its modern, radical wing. What we behold is the topical propaganda play, the didactic play, popular verse, the sociological novel, etc. The stalest wares of the communist outlook plus a noisy dash of pseudo-American jazz are mixed into a cocktail that burns but has no spirit. The strange and tragic fate of the German nation is inscrutably bound up with the compulsive propensity of the individual soul for a windowless loneliness and inwardness. Thence comes the sleep-drunk tendency to obedience, sometimes to the left and sometimes to the right. But thence also comes the tremendous genius of German music and poetry. - Berlin as the home of the muses is only a clamorous, illusory contrast trying to outshout the loneliness of the German character. The writer of the Enlightenment in 1770 (Nicolai and his sort) and the utilitarian writer of the present are identical down to the very last hair. Should the latter come upon the theme of "Faust," he probably would consider the Gretchen tragedy in terms of its polemical applicability against the statute which makes abortion illegal. Yesterday's fad known as the "new objectivity" is at bottom the "old unreality," only hypocritical. It is inverse romanticism which instead of moonlit ruins uses Chicago's skyscrapers for background.

In the field of education the omnipotent outlook of realism stands inflexibly opposed to spiritual re-awakening. To be sure, the elementary school has improved in recent years in the direction of direct naturalness and freedom. However, the basic motif of education is and remains the desire to rear only practical beings, that is, soulless beings oblivious to happiness.

In the major forces of modern civilized society, in the metropolitan press, theater, and cinema, the realistic outlook possesses its most powerful instruments. The daily vital question of these institutions is: "How can I today get below the level of yesterday"? In editorials, political claptrap is spewed forth in various shades of opinion. Everything else, with few notable exceptions, is "service to the customer." And this customer, whether news reader or auditor, is considered by those that serve him as the stupidest and most bigoted amoeba imaginable. Here, in the intellectual twilight of information and entertainment, the economic cycle of hyper-sophisticated stimuli and dull jadedness operates most repulsively, dominated by the fetichistic superstition that filth and worldly success are identical. Yes indeed, the superstitious belief in filth seems to be the religion of journalism and entertainment, the purveyance of filth, its ritual, the cheapness of the filth supply, its ethics. It never dreams that even the simplest individual is above such things and deserves something better. Let me amplify this charge by an example. When there is a dearth of genuine news, some spicy substitute must be created for the hungry reader. What happens?

Our contemporary gets up in the morning, reaches for the newspaper and is greeted with a roar by a six-inch headline, minus articles and verbs, somewhat as follows: CHICAGO TRUNK MYSTERY VICTIM FORMER ANGELINO. Thus every morning has its juicy murder in the pot. Cheap journalism sees to that, and the murderer whom it inspires. Joking aside, I am firmly convinced that without "modern" journalism there would be no "modern" underworld. It remained for the journalist to spread the world prominence of prize fighters and of criminals. And in contrast to this, the press shows its estimation of spiritual events by the modest headlines and the unsensational size of type on an inner page, that it devotes to them. There is a tacit and subtle collusion between book reviews and the size of the publisher's advertisement. But murder and sports are reported gratis in giant letters. Art is intangible and must consequently pay its way. Within the whole logical structure of the realistic outlook all of this is not astonishing. What is astonishing is that the few remaining civilized people do not get together in the printing plants of sensational filth and smash the rotary presses into smithereens.

Is it still necessary in this connection to recall the theater and the cinema? It is a matter of repeated experience that seriously intended plays above the common run are often well attended. Theater managers are then painfully surprised as a rule. Poor fellows! They no longer understand the world when such things happen. In the case of the cinema such miracles are virtually excluded from the outset. The powerful, moneyed cave men who control the motion pictures take good care that the natural economic law of cheapness is not upset. And yet, in the incomprehensible, polyphonic course of life's stream, the cinema and radio will perhaps play an unexpected role. Perhaps they will one day become the most powerful means of furthering the spiritual revolution against the belief in things alone. For it is the motion picture that stirs up the masses and the millions into a life of phantasy, that carries the thirst for dream and emotion to the lowest classes of society. It is the motion picture that has taught the most primitive people in Siberia and the South Seas really to know and graphically to experience the thrill of imaginative life.

A restoration of values! The history of the human race

is not the history of its manner of feeding, as modern superstition would have us believe, just as little as Schiller's or Walt Whitman's biography is the biography of his metabolism. No, it is and always will be the universal history of the shaping of the values and ideals that inwardly transform the material world. The heroic ideal produces feudalism and a substratum of slaves; the Christian-Catholic ideal restricts both of these to the life-form of the Gothic Middle Ages; the economic ideal of work of the rising bourgeois brings about, together with technical progress, proletarization, mass misery and, in consequence, social revolution, the age in which we now live. The transformation of values and ideals is always accomplished spasmodically and in a revolutionary manner. But that it is of a purely spiritual nature is proved each time by preceding history. So that Christianity might arise, it was necessary for the antinomian sectarianism of Judea to reach its apogee in Jesus and Paul. So that the bourgeois revolution might succeed, it was necessary for the Encyclopedists, Voltaire, and Rousseau to perform their work. So that the social revolution might come to pass, there had to be the great compassionate literature of misery of the nineteenth century, with Marx less important than Tolstoi and Zola. If, however, the spiritual man, the inwardly rich, unshakable, creative man of the muses is finally to have his turn and overthrow the realistic outlook, the preparation of this further revolution will require still greater effort and a more aggressive impulse.

Above all we must have the courage to disregard the prevailing fashion, even if as a result we ourselves are disregarded by the so-called spirit of the times. And

73

please, do not underestimate this courage! You will sooner be able to persuade a dandy in full-dress clothes to jump into the water than to get him to wear a black tie or tan shoes. And a radical dandy, a socialist fop, a communistic downward-snob or cynicism-dude will sooner herd sheep on Broadway than deny the truth of his all-conquering economic determinism. It is our task, however, beyond all vanity and at the risk of being denounced as reactionary, to imbue the world with the spiritual outlook. But before we can do this, we ourselves must first be imbued with our own belief. And what belief could be easier, freer, more undogmatic, more certain, more beatifying than the belief that, in spite of all material misery, the supreme goal of our happiness and existence is the unfolding and the intensification of the inner life?

Is the ocean as such anything wondrous? Are the Himalayas? Or a mountain lake? Or a forest? Let us assume we are not about five feet eight inches, but two thousand yards tall (an insignificant difference in the face of cosmic measurements); then the ocean would be a puddle of water to us, the Himalayas a mere threshold, and the forest a clump of grass. Or assume we were so clever that we could always and everywhere see the so-called real meaning behind all things. The ocean would then seem to us an extensive concentration of chemical constituents whose combination results in sea water; and the forest a matted brush of uninteresting blades of grass. In tree bugs and birds we should see a similar collection of insect parasites in the foliage. We could see nothing else in a beautiful face but the perfection of glandular secretion, and in spiritual endowment only a fortunate arrangement of physiological and social conditions.

But Heaven be praised, our soul is much too clever to be so clever. A beautiful face moves us ineffably; a great spiritual work forces us to our knees. A sombre valley fills us with grief; the ocean and the glacier, with singular terror.

Why are we frightened and by what? We are frightened by the miracle within us, by the muse that slumbers in every man, by God's messenger that repeats the work of creation each second. For the world begins in man. And man can only live in the name of the miracle.

Can We Live Without Faith in God?

The following pages contain the written text of an address and not the polished writing of a philosophical essay. Between the written and the spoken word the same distinction prevails as between the reading public and the listening public. The former constitutes an abstract community, the latter a highly concrete and perilous assemblage. The individual reader protects himself against the author by critical mistrust, the listener by lurking impatience. Whereas the one must be convinced, the other must be conquered. The rhetorical means of emphatic conveyance of thought is in sharp contrast to the literary obligation of deliberate presentation.

Fully aware of this antithesis, I have not revised my address in its printed version. There has been no polishing and no embellishment; the spontaneous formulation has received no subsequent props. Only a few interpolated notes serve the purpose of clarifying and strengthening the argument.

"There are more important questions."
(*Fritz Mauthner, under the entry "God"
in the "Philosophisches Woerterbuch."*)

"Watchman, what of the night?"
(*Isaiah, 21/11*)

I

When I chose the theme for this essay some time ago I had scarcely an inkling of the difficulties that lay in store for me. I thought it should be possible without further ado to give lucid expression to those thoughts and feelings that have become my inner property since early youth.

My sense of embarrassment is, consequently, all the greater now that I realize that nothing conceals itself more diffidently from words nor tends to remain more mute than the realm that I now venture to approach. Nor is that all. There is a deep and secret sore festering in the world. Its feverish pain is alleviated by the thick surgical dressings of modern philosophies and ideologies. Yet, whoever wishes to get to the bottom of things is compelled to approach this sore, to remove the dressings one by one and to palpate the edges of the infection. And in so doing he will arouse offense and anger; offense on the part of those who believe, but a far greater anger on the part of non-believers who furiously pounce upon anyone who, in a spirit of free inquiry, asks the great question of life. What an ironic commentary on the relativity of historical attitudes! The bigoted devotees of atheism and the slavish adherents of the materialistic outlook are at the present time the real representatives of intolerance.

Another difficulty which blocks my path is the question as to the legitimacy of my attempt. I am neither a theologian nor a clergyman. I cannot speak as a learned man, and still less as the accredited spokesman of a religion. By what right then do I presume to lay my finger on the sorest spot of modern mankind, by what right do I demand of my reader an hour of metaphysical deliberation? By no other right than that of our common situation in life. Both you and I come, by and large, from the same class of people; we have traversed similar paths of education; the same literature, science, and art has nourished us. Furthermore, our common situation in life, that of the educated middle class, lies midway between all parties and all views. I may therefore assume that the considerations which I shall present are not strange to you, and that my thoughts are the verbal expression of latent thoughts within you.

If a surveyor wishes to calculate the height of a towering peak, he must draw a base line from his position to some point of reference. I should like to determine such a base line between you and me in the sense that I shall not speak of formal religion nor of specific churches and faiths, but rather of the unconfined stream of metaphysics which today permeates the human soul as it always has and always will. Of this I shall speak, as well as of the tremendous and violent attempts of the prevailing spirit of worldliness to shut off the invisible rays of metaphysics. I am deliberately eliminating both boundary areas of my subject, the upper one of actual religion and the lower one of practical economic life. I merely mention this to protect myself against obvious objections. To be sure, Paul the Apostle warns us against such an intention which might lead to *apaideutas zeteseis,* undisciplined dialectic, to *logomachein* and *eutrapelia,* to hair-splitting and hypersophistication. We shall probably best avoid this danger if we remain aware of our own intellectual feebleness in the face of an inexhaustible theme and, as well as we can, strive for simplicity and subjective honesty.

II

Before me I see a street in a large city. It is not a central thoroughfare nor is it a street on the outskirts. It is an average street, not quite middle class and not quite proletarian. And it is also an average man whom I select from the hurrying throng at the close of business for the purpose of examining his soul under a magnifying glass.

If I had wanted to examine the character of the Middle Ages, I should have had to detain a meditating monk; and if it were a question of comprehending the Renaissance, I would choose a prince; - the symbol of our day, however, is not the man of high position but the average man. He is the actual subject and object of democracy, the true bearer of our history.

This bearer of contemporary world history is, moreover, a man of middle age. His profession? A small business man, a city employee, a teacher... If one takes into consideration the worn and listless facial expression, the most probable diagnosis would be "a poorly paid individual with a steady job." I once knew that man. During the war we had once spent several weeks in the very same barracks room. A conversation springs up and only lasts from one street corner to the next. This brief exchange is enough to enable me without any particular effort of imagination to reproduce completely in my mind the man's mental state and his spiritual constitution. I can relate the story of his inner life, so clearly is it spread before me, day by day, from childhood on.

He was an average child like a hundred thousand others, neither more nor less spiritual than anyone else. Up to his seventh year, he was afraid of the dark, as all children are. In the darkness of his small bedroom the supernatural powers of the entire universe converged, and he lay there facing them alone. Even before he could name them as spirits, angels and devils, these words were astir in his blood as the inherited awe carried down through hundreds of generations. His mother often took the child with her to church. And here, at the sound of the organ and in the glow of the candles, he experienced quite other types of holy feelings of awe, which the grown man, strangely enough, forgot more completely than his fear of the demonic darkness.

When the boy, now of school age, still showed himself to be timorous, his father soundly boxed his ears one day. And on the heels of this act followed the moral: "Spirits, angels, devils and other superstitions do not exist," explained the father; "the world is an entirely natural affair; its chief purpose consists in not remaining too long a burden to harassed parents, and in earning one's own living as soon as possible." My little man of the crowd thus received his first conclusive enlightenment concerning the natural, scientific character of the world and its purely economic purpose. His early insight into the needy circumstances of his parents' home, the faces of his father and mother constantly shadowed by care, these and other things bolstered the work of education. School continued the process despite weekly lessons in religion and Sunday exhortations.

However, at the age of sixteen or seventeen even this poor average man experienced something in the nature of a spiritual crisis. He suddenly began to read avidly everything that he could lay his hands on. It was no accident that Ernst Haeckel's "Riddle of the Universe" fell into his hands. In this book there was a particularly bright passage that determined the philosophy of our young man. I quote it from memory: "In reality even this immaterial spirit is not conceived of as incorporeal but as invisible, gaseous. This anthropomorphism leads to the paradoxical representation of God as a so-called 'gaseous vertebrate.'" This struck home like a flash of lightning.

The period of frenzied reading, of course, lasted only a short while, for his occupation and his indolence quickly exhausted the lazy mind of my acquaintance. From the days of his Faustian striving he retained in his head only a tired midges' dance of jumbled concepts: all sorts of vague and distorted notions, about the origin of species, and man's unparadisiac past as an ape, about the atomic structure of matter, about thought as a function of the brain centers, and more of the like. If we wished to reduce all these fractional bits of knowledge to the common denominator of a philosophical conviction, it would go as follows:

Our man believes that reality is identical with his sensual world of experience. In accordance with this he believes, moreover, that it is a purely material world, springing out of itself and providing its own purpose. The spiritual forces in it are by-products of its internal metabolism and, within the economy of the whole, these forces at most play the role of lubricating oil in a machine. Indeed, man knows not why he is in the world; however, since he is there he must adjust himself to it. And this is best done by employing technological means to reduce the possibilities of suffering. This is called progress.

Now of course, our average man cannot think so conclusively, nor can he formulate his thoughts with such skill. As a matter of fact, he no longer thinks at all. For a long time he has been indifferent to all these questions because he has other worries: a shrewish wife, two sons with radical leanings, and a poorly paid position from which he may be dismissed any day and be left without a pension. Nevertheless he is completely permeated by the conviction described above. It constitutes his unconscious state of consciousness, so to speak. It is filtered into his brain by a thousand apparent and secret ways. Every moving-picture program conveys it to him. It exists as an under-current in the intonation of every conversation. It is injected into him twice a day by his favorite newspaper, regardless of its politics. And even if it were a religious publication it could not do otherwise.

As the result of his entire course of development he cannot believe in the Divine, to which he is bound only by certain ritual occasions, and in which he is involved as a citizen and head of a family: christenings, confirmations, marriages, funerals, cheerful or somber meetings from which he returns home with indigestion and frost-bitten feet.

However, I shall not conceal the fact that my acquaint-ance, in later years, was once more afflicted by a mental shock. He once happened to pick up an old scrap of news-paper containing an article on astronomy and soon was engrossed in it. In this article the astronomer expatiated on the ridiculously thin veil which matter represents in the void of universal space. He then went on to speak of the millions and millions of fixed stars which constitute 99/100ths of matter, a fact involving the entire cosmic time-space drama. If we now consider, continued the astronomer, that all these fixed stars are white-hot gas-eous bodies glowing at inconceivably high temperatures, and if we further consider that, among all the milky ways and astral nebulae, earthlike planets sustaining or-ganic life can only be formed with infinitesimal rarity, then it is obvious that this organic life, including the human species, is not in the least the supreme purpose of the universe. On the contrary, it is an accidental resi-due of matter, a phenomenon of its decay, a minor splash, a type of parasitic disease or skin infection of the uni-verse.

This anti-human astronomy dealt the man a no less violent blow than Haeckel's "gaseous vertebrate" had once dealt the boy. Crushed, and filled with the stifling sensation of dark futility, he crept away. In another age another person might have carried away the opposite im-pression of this cosmological interpretation. He might possibly have seen in it a corroboration of the classical hypothesis, to wit, that our tiny planet and its humans are the great exception and the center of the universe. But this bright and bold conception is forbidden by the modern state of consciousness that I have already described.

Meanwhile our acquaintance has long forgotten the depressing newspaper article. For some time now he has not been the carefree stroller and friend of nature that he used to be, which incidentally is one of his best traits. He has become strangely sad, even melancholy. This has nothing to do with his worries about earning a living and caring for his family, nor with the physical changes to which a man of about fifty is subject. I believe I know exactly the secret of this melancholy. It is called the fear of death. Yes, the man is afraid of death. Visions of suffering before death, the terrifying images of dissolution and of decay take possession of his soul with increasing morbidity, although he does not openly acknowledge it to himself, and goes about his business, following his usual routine. Primarily it is the hidden yet boundless fear of fatal illness, of the instant of death, of physical dying. But is there for him anything more than the physical? That is it precisely. Behind the fear of physical destruction lurks a second, far more profound fear of death. It might argue thus in the mind of our perplexed friend if he were not too obtuse:

"Here I am, begotten by two chance parents, one chance night, for the purpose of a doubtful pleasure. And suddenly I woke up in this world and existed. What followed was about four-fifths want and unhappiness (domestic distress, drudgery, war, sickness, death) and one-fifth moderate gratification (food, drink, a few furtive escapades, a game of cards, walking and an occasional pleasure trip). Nevertheless, little as it was, it was far from being nothing. After all, I did have something. And I became so fond of that something that I love nothing else, for it is I myself, my ego. My wife gets on my nerves, my sons are wicked scoundrels, my job is a treadmill, - it is only my ego that I love, nothing else. And now my dear ego is to be taken from me, not in gentle sleep but in fearful convulsions. What a monstrous sentence of judgment without appeal! In the beginning I was nothing. Then I acquired an ego clamoring for pleasure and sensitive to pain, only to have it taken from me. And in the end, I not only again become nothing, but a poignant nothing, a nothing minus my ego."

By now we know that our man on the street is incapable of thinking. But these conclusions which I have just drawn fill his soul with dark, nebulous anguish, even if he cannot put them into words. He isolates himself more and more every day and acquires the reputation of a grouchy eccentric. But he is only a profoundly unhappy man. And now he begins to recall his mother and the day she died. She had departed gently under the protection of faith. His remembrance of her fills him with strange solace and strange envy.

Many people claim never to have known the fear of death or of dissolution. Such freedom from fear, however, might be less attributed to bravery than to a sluggish imagination. For the existence of a feeling and the becoming aware of it are two different things. Anyone who has been exposed to battle or to great danger knows that in the intensified moments of imminent death an intoxicated feeling of exhilaration makes the world unreal and thus does away with fear. It is the nature of this fear to be numbed by extreme trial and activity. But its manner is different if we are drifting along on the placid stream of everyday life. He who does not pause in introspection nor stop to reflect with awe on death, dissolution, and eternity, either consciously or unconsciouly, - though he may in other respects be an excellent living creature, is not a human being. The spirit of the times does everything in its constant turmoil and noise to keep man's great finalities out of his consciousness. Nevertheless, these finalities cannot be wholly repressed, as even my average man on the street demonstrates.

III

Naturally I have not introduced my man of the crowd in order to present a literary study of character. No, he serves only as an embodied symbol for the presentation of that all-pervading modern state of consciousness which I shall call *naturalistic nihilism*. Just as there still exists a strong popular faith in wide areas there also exists a strong popular skepticism. It is embodied in the anonymous man of the metropolis whom I am portraying. Let us, once again, define this naturalistic, nihilistic mental and spiritual constitution by expressing the monstrosity in conceptual terms:

In accordance with this view, all life, including personal life, is a pleasurable and unpleasurable interruption of the unconscious void. Nature, as far as we comprehend it, represents a soulless mechanism of forces which either balance or destroy each other, a sort of permanent catastrophe held in abeyance. Man plays the part of the "Man in Syria leading a camel by the halter rope," as in Rueckert's fable. Perhaps you may recall the story of the poor camel driver who, fleeing from the enraged animal, took refuge in a well in the depths of which lurked a dragon; and the harried victim, threatened by the camel above him, clung to a bramble bush whose roots were being gnawed by a black mouse and a white mouse in turn, the symbols of day and night. Culture is a constant war of position against the brute forces of nature outside and inside of man, with technology its main weapon. There is no possibility of approaching a higher meaning of the universe by knowledge or sensation. For, in the first place, our sensual apparatus of perception is as inadequate as our reason in the attainment of absolute knowledge; and, in the second place, such a meaning of the universe is *per se* an anthropomorphic subsumption and an empty figure of speech. As for the so-called religious feelings, they have long ago been exposed by our extremely smug modern psychology as infantile residues, both in the individual and in society.

Such, in very brief outline, is the philosophy of naturalistic nihilism, the popular philosophy which has become part of the flesh and blood of European, Russian, and American metropolitan populations. Though there still may be many millions of positive believers in the world, it is not they who determine the living spirit of the age but the nihilism just described.

In a previous essay I attempted to lay bare the historical, economic, and psychological roots of the modern realistic outlook. Now I shall probe for its deepest root, its root of the metaphysical.

It would be an enticing venture to draw the line that runs from Thomas Aquinas to Karl Marx, from the Church's pre-established plan of history and salvation to historical materialism. However, I must forego all historical interpolation since our inquiry concerns only the present epoch. Of course, even with reference to the history of religion, our present epoch dates back to the beginning of the eighteenth century, as does the entire realistic outlook.

Naturalistic nihilism has come a long way and has left many milestones behind it. Each of these milestones signified a new severance of man from his metaphysical ties. The knife with which he severed the mystical threads between his heart and the Divine was given to him by natural science. The accomplishments of science were so prodigious, the vistas which it exposed to weak mortal eyes since Galileo, Kepler and Newton were so overpowering that we can very well understand why man, in his exuberant intoxication of knowledge, considered himself master of the universe, and why he forgot the deepest secret of creation in the face of so many apparently solved riddles. The human spirit, blinded by the telescope and microscope, for a time grew blind to God, a fact in which, perhaps, is concealed some inscrutable intention of the scheme of history. Not until the World War (1914-18) did nihilism reach its climax; as a result of the war and during its course, nihilism attained its completion.

Once again we turn our attention to the mediocre man of the crowd, the average man of the city. He belongs to one of the war generations. In the World War he not only lost his health but the last remainder of the ideals implanted in him by the state. As we have seen, he possesses only one thing in this world, his poor beloved ego. And unfortunately he becomes aware of his ego only as a chain of depressing circumstances: worry about his pension, the deep-seated fear of death, a vague bitterness, a boundless feeling of loneliness, incipient vascular deterioration and gout. He is as completely shorn of universal affinity as ever a man was. And the same is true of the greater part of his generation. The World War was, in a higher sense, an admonition that things could no longer go on as they were.

And things did not go on as they were. The man of the absolute void is incapable of living. The very statement proves the fact. A change occurred that forms an important link in our argument. Our man has two sons, twenty and twenty-one years old. These young men will not and cannot live with a passive, regimented ego which is only the void on temporary leave. They are striving violently to get away from their ego. Although they are very poor, perhaps poorer than any youthful generation has ever been before, they do not resign themselves,—an activity which has completely occupied their father up to this time. They are seeking a connection with a higher order, a super-order, an authority to which they can passionately subject themselves, and for which, if occasion arises, they can sacrifice their lives. World history teaches us that man cheerfully offers his life only for one thing, for his faith. Our time offers the young men two radical types of faith. No doubt you have already guessed that one son of our man of the street is a communist and the other a national socialist. Naturalistic nihilism splits into two branches, as it were. Youth takes a step away from the helpless ego. Communism and national socialism are primitive stages in the conquest of the ego. They are substitute religions or, if you will, substitutes for religion.

IV

We must establish the fact that theoretical communism is not a type of knowledge, as it alleges, but a type of faith. It juggles logical categories in order to thrust ahead to its *credo quia absurdum*. Its very fundamental doctrine is pure dogma, that is, the doctrine which proclaims that the origin of, and key to, all things human is socialization for the purpose of the production of goods. The means of life as an end of life is a time-bound notion typical of the mechanistic nineteenth century.

F. A. Lange writes in his "History of Materialism": "Adam Smith, the creator of political economy, reduced the play of interests, the market traffic of supply and demand, to rules which even today have not lost their significance. Nevertheless, to Adam Smith this market of interests was not the whole of life, but only an important aspect of it. His successors, however, forgot the opposite aspect and confused the rules of the market with the rules of life, indeed, with the principles of human nature. This error, moreover, aided in giving political economy a gloss of strict scientific objectivity by bringing about a significant simplification of all problems. However, this simplification consists in men being thought of as purely egoistic and as beings who know to perfection how to look after their special interests without ever being hindered by other sentiments."

CAN WE LIVE WITHOUT FAITH IN GOD?

To make economics, a very late phenomenon of life, the point of departure for the study of history is entirely arbitrary. We know that among primitive people the life of law and of ritual played a vastly greater role than economic logic.

Economics! - that hardworking woman lost her head at her sudden rise in status. Since her high priests have elevated into general colloquial speech the liturgical mystic words of barter, terms like "rediscount," "below par," "frozen credits," - this she-devil has afflicted us with plague and drought. There is many a philosophy of history but none has yet shown us that historical reality, for the greater part, is caused by words and slogans.

The second main doctrine of communism appears no less windy with its theory of the so-called "ideological superstructure." Consciousness, the intellectual life of man, is neither more nor less than a function of his social situation. Since this situation, however, is so constituted that some are in possession of the means of production whereas the others are not, and since, in accordance with this, there exist only exploiters and exploited, all intellectual products are nothing else but the subtle means of justification of the exploiter class in order that it might be able to continue maintaining its privileged status forever. Thus, in this sense, the God of the bible is a crafty invention of the rich Hebrews for the purpose of keeping the poor Hebrews in check; Shakespeare's Hamlet together with his dynastic scandal of poisoning and adultery is the unconscious attempt to safeguard the large estates of feudalism. In short, the totality of world literature from Hammurabi to Joyce is always an opiate for the purpose of preventing the given proletariat of the epoch from awakening. I say this not to be facetious, for similar ideas are actually being asserted by world-famous authors.

But it is the communist dogma concerning the great finalities of life and the classless society that makes the greatest demand on faith.

The saviors, it is claimed, will be the proletariat. ("Why," asks reason, "should it be the most retarded class of people? Are we not here also confronted by an ideological superstructure, or better, a psychological substructure of *bourgeois* hatred of itself?") Since there will be no more exploited, the claim goes on, those subtle intellectual forces which had only formed the protection of master privileges will disappear, above all, religion in every form.

In the classless society, it is further claimed, the cycle of production and consumption will be completely controlled. Thus, for the first time in history man will be independent of the compulsion of inanimate things which he will now completely master. For the first time he will come into his own, for the first time he will gain a free awareness of himself for all time and eternity.

However large may be the amount of *credo quia absurdum* that is imputed to the faithful believer, it cannot be denied that something strange and attractive emanates from this latter doctrine. Primeval overtones, messianic, apostolic certainty of the imminent Kingdom of Heaven echo forth from the depths of history. It is the image of Paradise Regained, where lion and lamb dwell peacefully side by side.

The true communist will smile scornfully at such comparisons. He considers himself a rationalist to the very core. But it is precisely a clear rationalism that must confront him with the following:

All historical life is of a dynamic nature, that is, a rhythmic sequence of mutually contradictory states. "Man must be destroyed again and again," is one of Goethe's profoundest sayings. And indeed, history is only a part of organic life and, in its own way, repeats life's two-cycle process: inhaling-exhaling, construction-destruction, birth-death. A cultural endeavor to perpetuate a definite state of society, though it be the most just, is utopian. There are at work in mankind dark destructive forces of instinct instituted by nature so that change might not be interrupted. Consequently there is, in reality, no such thing as salvation in this world. A geologist has calculated that our planet guarantees humanity an adequate existence for many hundred millions of years, provided there is no cosmic collision to spoil matters. Should the classless society break out in about the year 2033, a society which for all future time will eliminate the individual's lust for power, his lust for possession, his bellicose instinct, his sadistic delusion of asserting authority, one would still be unable to avoid the anxious question: "And what happens in the remaining 398 million years?"

All the above dreams are based on the liberal superstition of rectilinear progress, of a constant higher development of mankind, and in addition, on the dogmatic and fundamental error that economics makes man, and not man economics.

Moreover, an unbridgeable contradiction gapes between the notion of a classless society as an economic final goal and the so-called historical-dialectical concept which is supposed to guarantee the achievement of this final goal. Dialectic is an incessant mechanism of life and can only end with life itself. Since, however, economics shapes the external social form of this mechanism, the idea of its complete control, i.e. suspension, signifies an unconscious metaphysical belief. The believer in Marx, when such matters are pointed out to him, generally retreats to the point of view that within a good theory the practical way is more important than a "hazy final goal." However, in thus surrendering the supreme dogma of his theory of salvation, he devalues it into the mere combat action of a class, the human meaning of which, as in every military operation, is extremely questionable.

No argument, however, can convert a communist since he is a fanatical believer. This is additional confirmation of the fact that communism represents a substitute for religion with a scientific mask of reason, a primitive heresy in the guise of political economy. Thus the only ones to take it seriously were a comparatively religious people. The Russians might be said to be in the same position today that the West occupied in the twelfth and thirteenth centuries. The Russian people are now experiencing their Gothic Middle Age, the fervent longing for the realization of the thousand-year empire, of course with the content and form of our time.

But beware! Let no one think that these ideas provide a refuge for reactionary interests. The Marxist doctrine is undoubtedly false and perverse. But the social and economic reality of our day is just as false, perverse, and unbearable. The secular conflict between labor and the machine, the struggle for human leisure, by which the mystery of the future is to be established, these do not belong in the frame of the present study. However, it must be admitted that of all political evils, that is the least which fights, though with unsuitable means, for the secret of the future. Though socialism is militantly anti-religious, the true religious spirit, nonetheless, can only be deeply socialistic. This is one of the great contradictions which will never be understood by a political numbskull, who in matters of decision sees only partisanship, and in partisanship already sees the decision.

The fact that strict realization of Christianity presupposes a communistic community-life does not have to be confirmed. The fullness and clarity of the Evangelical Word undoubtedly demands it. Surrender, renunciation, and sacrifice here have, of course, another, suprasocial sense. They do not set up the general welfare as an ultimate goal and value, but the spiritualization and divine perfection of the personality.

At any rate, the communist son of our man on the street does not take his cause lightly. He is a workingman, a mechanic in a factory. Very soon he will be unemployed. He attends meetings; he belongs to the advance guard; he studies the party literature He is shaken by a fanatical urge to run away from the father within himself, and also by the martial longing to be consumed in some general flame. Who knows whether it is not a decisive step into the materialistic hell that is the first step leading out of it?

V

Matters are different with the younger son.

Most of us have at some time attended a football game.

It presents an extremely instructive sight. A mass of sixty thousand people, head to head, fused together into a circular monster. This monster, fascinated and ready to erupt, is staring down into the arena where two teams are fighting it out. One of these teams belongs to the monster; it represents the cause of the monster's city or state. This is supposed to be only a game. But you hear a primitive roar, a frenzied clatter of victory when one of our men makes a goal. And when the umpire lets an opponent's foul go unpenalized, you hear an ear-splitting "Boo-o-o-o!" like the foghorns of twenty giant ocean liners. But if the opponents score a success a deathly silence reigns, interrupted only by the half-hearted applause of a few renegades and defeatists. No generosity to the enemy!

At every great international match, in the midst of the immense crowd, you can experience the essence of nationalism; indeed, as a particle of the mass you can scarcely escape the intoxication of victory. The sight of the raging monster shows us that nationalism is not some imagined theory but a dark, gigantic emotion in which the collective vanity of the mass and its aroused will to assertion are gratified. In contrast to this, the so-called class consciousness of the proletariat is a demon which is far less deeply rooted, because the mass which it represents is bound together more by purpose than by blood. The greatest success of Soviet politics lies in the art with which it directs the two streams of feeling into the same channel.

It is very easy for nationalism to serve as a substitute for religion. Nationalism is an emotion which scarcely costs anything, for the credit of belonging to a nation is only dependent on the achievement of being born. Any nonentity at least belongs somewhere. Nationalism raises biological membership to a moral value. It awards the individual, tax-free, a medal of bravery for all the historical victories and great deeds of his people. Furthermore, it grants ecstatic experience to youth, permits it credulously to incorporate its ego into a higher system, into a nobler transcendent order.

It would be denying the value of man if one wished to deprive nations of their value. Individual, family, and nation are organic, God-given, fundamental facts of life. The secret of creature values, however, consists in their truly being able to blossom only in the realm of naiveté, and in their gradual fading in the realm of self-consciousness. So, too, a woman is beautiful in the purest sense only as long as she does not know that she is beautiful. If consciousness enters, beauty is poisoned by vanity. Similarly, a nation retains its creature value only as long as it is not poisoned by nationalism, that is, by vain and aggressive self-consciousness.

However that may be, communism demands of its adherents a few moral and scientific insights; it is vibrant with the thought of justice for the deliverance of mankind. In contrast, nationalism is nothing but a reaction of feeling, a dark impulse, a powerful upheaval, and does not pretend to be anything else. If communism, as a substitute for religion, can be compared, let us say, with an early Christian heresy, then nationalism is comparable to heathenism and the pagan outlook. As the herald of primordial forces of existence, nationalism disdains to argue; it speaks like an oracle. Its favorite notion is a nebulous concept of "life" as a last fearful resort, beyond good and evil, at once beautiful and terrible, which can best be served in the form of war-like, armed units. (We must not forget that its father is called nihilism.) Nationalism, to be sure, considers itself a proclaimer of severity and directness; yet it can never in all the world work its way out of the realm of the indefinite and the flabby. The intellectual atmosphere it breathes is the slogan. One should not underestimate the power of the slogan. It serves not as truth but as magic incantation. He who is most deeply permeated by it is entitled to leadership. Consequently, the best equipment for a radically nationalistic leader is self-assured ambiguity and a suggestive smattering of culture. The stock of ideas of hostile parties is unscrupulously looted and the plundered words twisted into resounding and emotional phrases. Instead of the former "disappropriation of capital," the national socialist threatens "the smashing of interest-slavery." In the foreground the so-called mercenary troopers scurry about, foolhardy adventurers, true visionaries of heroism, confused or frustrated talents who are gambling on a new order, - but in the background, as the actual bearer of nationalistic emotion, stands the stubborn mass of disillusioned, impoverished, and enraged petty bourgeois.

Xenophobia is the name given to the fear and hatred of everything foreign. The petty bourgeois fears and hates everything foreign. He does not know the world and therefore he shuns and detests it. He loves the smell of his own room and considers it incomparable. That is why he raves about "Germanization" or "Italianization." He importunes anthropology in order to prove that his race excels all others. Everyone knows that the European is a motley mixture in contrast to whom any stray mongrel might feel like a pedigreed animal. But slogans and incantations create realities that do not exist. All of this denotes an insolent, blasphemous hypostasis of the body as the only divinity, and conceals behind pompous and inflated words the miasmic abyss of lost mental and spiritual health.

All mass feelings are eminently of a feminine nature. Hence the hysterical adoration of war-like manliness by nationalistic emotion, and hence also the Megaera-like searching for parts of the population or for persons who must bear all blame.

No matter how one tries to circumscribe the meaning of nationalism, it exists as a powerful force; its roots are in the vanity of nations; it is without argument and hence cannot be affected by argument. Youth, weary of its paternal nihilism, lays wreaths upon the altar of nationalism. The *"absurdum"* only intensifies youth's *"credo."*

The younger son of our man on the street devotes every free day to secret terrain exercises in preparation for a new war of vengeance. Since he finds no footing in the world, he voluntarily chooses military drill, just as, for lack of true faith, he secretly and voluptuously cherishes in his heart a strange hope for the destruction of the world.

VI

We have thus demonstrated that the two greatest movements of the present, communism and nationalism, are anti-religious, albeit religion-substituting, types of faith, and by no means merely political ideals. They are true children of the nihilistic epoch and hence bear a marked resemblance to their parent. Like their father they know no transcendent affinity; like him they are suspended in a vacuum. However, they are no longer satisfied with this vacuum but create pandemonium in it so as to destroy it.

Communism and nationalism are the chief idols. But there are ever so many lesser idols. One of the most favored is technology. (I am here considering it as a spiritual, not as an economic factor). Since there is only this material world here below, it soon becomes too constricted for us. So let us be off on our aerial rocket into universal space! What unmitigated *hybris!* We humans, we planetary creatures have no license to emigrate physically. We hop about like captive fleas in a closed box. If we succeed in hopping up into the stratosphere of this box, we are beside ourselves with arrogance. But let us calm down! With one glance into the night sky our eyes take in millions of light-years. We can penetrate the cover of the box with our minds and hearts, not with our skulls.

Another idol whose adoration is demanded by nationalism is the State. It is claimed that the present democratic and parliamentary State is to blame for all evil. Only the dictatorship of the elite, of the purest breed, would transform it from a pigsty of corruption into a temple of purity. Again a *credo quia absurdum.* What is the truth of the matter? The modern State is the resultant of both the genuine and the whipped-up desires of competing masses of voters, intensified by the vampirism of the State apparatus which sucks dry those it is supposed to serve. The whip-wielders and beneficiaries of the voters' desires are called politicians. Democracy is the corruption of the ones divided by the corruption of the others. Dictatorship is the armed monopolization of the pork barrel and of political power, exercised by a single party.

From what has been said it becomes clear that the exercise of power, when controlled by an opposition, affords a relatively better form of State than the unauthorized and unhindered rule of those usurpers who spring triumphantly out of latent or open civil war. The misery of States is not dependent upon economic and political destinies alone but just as much on their ruling personalities and their interests. However, within the spiritual and moral order of rank, the type of human being who strives for power is generally on a rather low level. In view of this circumstance a better State could only arise if, on the one hand, the passion for power were to be strictly separated from government and if, on the other hand, the representation of a people were to be withdrawn from demagogues and ward heelers and placed into the hands of spiritual personalities.

But enough! I have no desire to continue the casuistics of the void. In its preoccupation with the old, barren parliamentary geography of Right and Left, the world has forgotten that there is an Above and a Below. And since everything social ultimately depends on man, it is here that we find the very deepest reason for what has long been called "the crisis." It is truly a crisis of confidence. The hidden gold backing of spiritual currency has disappeared. A competitive hell of demonized interests surrounds us. I have already attempted to show the external way in which this came about. Here we are concerned only with its spiritual significance.

I have already mentioned the discovery of undreamed-of facts of nature in recent centuries, facts by means of which some broad perspectives were opened and others blocked up. For a pocket watch held in front of the eye can hide a mountain.

The crowding together of people into cities of millions has done its share. In the city man loses his importance as a universal being. Such is, in a spiritual sense, the secret aim of large cities. That is why they were of necessity built up in the time of increasing nihilism, which is the state of consciousness of the bourgeois-capitalistic epoch. Cities are places of escape, full of secret corners into which one can comfortably crawl away to hide from the deeper reality of life. Here, in workshops, in offices, moving-picture theaters and night clubs, man overcomes the thunderous realization of what he truly is and what he is not, on his journey through starry infinity on the roaring wings of the ether. He overcomes his sense of worship that should force him to his knees; he overcomes the fear of guilt within him which is deeper than the fear of death. The nihilistic secret of the large city is that it makes everything seem a matter of course. If spirituality is the rapturous shock at the everyday miracle of life, the large city banishes that spirituality. Day and night become a matter of course. The world cannot be seen for the people in it. Space becomes the inside of an office; time becomes a working hour for which one is paid, or an hour of amusement for which one must pay. By this matter-of-course atmosphere, in which primeval astonishment (the *thau-*

mazein of Aristotle) is extinguished, our strong spiritual powers are lulled to sleep until they fade out into an indifferent cynicism. The monastery of Athos is no place of escape from the world, but New York, Berlin, Paris and London are.

Behind the narcotic fog of the daily whirl squats the cruel fear of death that we have met in our symbolic man of the crowd. More than the fear of death, it is the fear of the *void*. Like the disease of cancer it causes metastases that constantly erupt in different form at other points of the social body. A blood-curdling shriek for security in life is now rending the air of cities, shrill as never before. Life wants to secure itself against the void that is raging within it. The risk of the eternal void is to be met by the premium of temporal insurance. Increasingly the idea of the State is assuming the character of an insurance company. Social security, old age pension, pension legislation, sickness compensation plans, etc., - all these institutions are secretly based on the conception that being born is a calamity for which State and Society must be obliged to award compensation. This conception corresponds entirely with the temper of naturalistic nihilism. It springs no less from metaphysical despair than from material misery.

The world of the rich has become a sanatorium world. In every direction it teems with the mystics of health cults, the yogis of cosmetics, the prophets of rejuvenation and the fakirs of metabolism. The triumph of the last mentioned with their gospel of the intestine, exceeds even that of the rejuvenators' monkey glands. Raw-food vegetarians and those of the leguminous school are rapidly going out of style; prune days are giving way to potato days; and it is to be expected that the belly-worshiping snobs will soon have to resign themselves to herring-scale days or cactus-needle treatments in order to remain in the lead. Since there is no eternal affinity the temporal bond is torn. Deaf to love and kinship, one ego rushes breathlessly past the other. What remains is misery and crime. When I think of daily murders and of corpses found here and there, I am convinced that capital punishment is a useless remedy. The re-establishment of eternal punishment in hellfire would be far more useful.

Apocalyptic pictures have been painted by many moralists. The question as to what we should do, as to where lies the path of righteousness is not new, for everyone asks this question of himself in troublous hours. The answer to this question is not only old, but the oldest of all: When all paths are blocked then only the path to Heaven remains. - Men of faith, of whom there are more on all levels of culture than is believed, regard this answer as no Popish catchword. It is easy for such people because the path stands open for them. The others, however, who have strayed into the blind alley of naturalistic nihilism and the realistic outlook, must first be made to realize that there can be no human life without transcendental affinity, and that even their skepticism is but a perverted faith without salvation.

The favorite means of combat employed by the skeptic against religious facts is a trick of logic by means of which he diverts inquiry about the Creator into the genetic and psychological sphere and identifies Divinity with man's conception of God: "Look! they have worshiped fetishes and phalli, idols with the heads of dogs and bulls, and are still doing it in a subtler form to this very day! So abstruse do their gods appear!" This nonsense can be easily disposed of.

Some Papuan negroes, for example, consider the stars to be very large and distant fireflies. Does this circumstance by any chance argue against the real existence of the stars as stars? No! It only argues against the literal imagination of those Papuan negroes. Psychoanalysis asserts that the human thought of God is the fruit of a prehistoric, infantile father-complex. However, if psychoanalysis infers from this assertion that the existence of a Divine Being is a compulsion-neurosis illusion carried down from primitive times, it thereby commits an unpardonable error of logic. Establishing the existence of this father-complex may possibly have relevance as regards the psychic life of the child, but none whatsoever as regards the existing or non-existing reality of the father. Without belittling its other merits, we can see that is it psychoanalysis rather than God which is a compulsion neurosis.

The assumption of the father-complex as the origin of the human conception of God is, furthermore, an arbitrary restriction of the history of religion. The fairly recent epoch of patriarchal veneration was preceded by a long and obscure age of matriarchal deities. Bachofen writes in the preface to his *"Mutterrecht"*—"The fame of having given to the Zeus-like nature of fatherdom its purest development cannot be taken from the Attic race. Even though Athens rests upon Pelasgian nationality, it has, nonetheless, subordinated the Demetrian principle to the Apollinian." In accordance with this, the father-complex is a rather young, one might almost say, a *bourgeois* phenomenon. The idea of God is incomparably older than the patriarchate. But both matriarchal and patriarchal deities are only time-bound interpretations of a single creative principle. They irresistibly corroborate the fact that humanity possesses an inner realization of this principle before, and no matter how, it interprets it.

In the same vicious circle as psychoanalysis moves every history of religion and philosophy that denies the the existence of God. The famous freethinker and philosopher, Ludwig Feuerbach, says in his lectures: "If Hobbes derives the understanding from the ears because he identifies the understanding with the audible word, one can, with greater justification, on the basis of the fact that thunder drove home to man the belief in gods, define the eardrum as the sounding board of religious feeling, and the ear as the womb of the gods." This observation denotes nothing else than the fact that the ear is man's numenal organ, a fact which the mystics already knew 5,000 years ago. But how in the world does this prove that it is not a metaphysical reality which corresponds to the prophetic perceptions which this organ awakens in our soul? Are thunder and the forces of nature no longer miracles since school children have learned to babble about electric discharges? *"Primus in orbe deos fecit timor."* True enough! But why did fear create the gods, of all things, and not storm-proof shelters? Can it perhaps be that lightning rods on top of churches have made the churches superfluous? - "God is a primeval father-complex." "The fear of thunder created the Deity!" Such sentences are downright tautologies. They assert that the contents of perception are primarily not *real* but merely *psychic* facts, a denunciation that says nothing.

The content of perception of the Divine in the human soul can neither be denied nor debased by psychological hypotheses as to how this content came into being historically. Such hypotheses are exposed upon closer scrutiny as *a priori* arguments swayed by feeling, arguments which are not designed to give truth its due but rather to promote some specific, and in the broadest sense, political outlook. The origin of atheism is not the *knowledge* that God does not exist but the *wish* that He might not exist. Consequently, the atheist primarily and always betrays only his own psychology when he thinks he is unveiling the mystery; and his denial unwittingly becomes the proof of God by confirming, against his own troubled will, the tremendous and vital importance of the metaphysical content of perception.

We shall endeavor, by means of a little parable, to describe the role which this content of perception plays in our soul. From physiology we know that the living matter in our sense organs has become so specialized that our sense organs yield to all stimuli only a single, innate response. If, for example, in the case of a blind man, the outer eye has been destroyed but the optical nerve is uninjured, this nerve, stimulated by pressure, will arouse vivid sensations of light in the blind man's mind without any accompanying objective perception of light. In other words, in the cells of the optical nerve, the perception of light has been produced in a mysterious way independent of the reality of light. In an even far more mysterious way—(please don't forget that we are speaking in terms of a parable)—a perception of the Divine has been produced in the spiritual totality of man, a perception which points to the supersensual reality of this Divine, just as the blind man's inner sensation of light points to what is for him the supersensual reality of light.

Descartes' opinion in this matter is somewhat as follows: From whence do we have the idea of God? The fact that every idea must have a cause follows from the clear and distinct axiom: nothing can come from nothing. From this it also follows that the cause may not contain less reality than the effect, for the increase would then have come out of nothing. The idea of God has not come to me by way of the senses, nor have I formed it myself. The capacity to conceive of a more perfect Being than myself I can only have from Someone who is more perfect than I. - The idea of God is my original possession; it is as innately in me as the idea of myself. Limited as it may be, it is still sufficient to realize the fact of God's existence, although not to understand His Being; just as one might touch a mountain without being able to embrace it.

If so many people today no longer know this inner perception, that does not mean it has died out in them but merely shows that atheistic nihilism has, by means of suggestion, paralyzed that point of the consciousness where this inner perception makes itself felt.

However, I do not propose to waste any time on the criticism of atheism and prefer to turn my attention to that science which leads us beyond all psychology, to the science of matter, the science of the universe, to the most exact of all sciences, to physics. Physics has experienced a tremendous revolution in the last thirty years. Prior to this revolution, as a fixed, mechanistic physics, it acted as the guarantor of naturalistic nihilism. Filled with the arrogance of a clever engineer, it fancied itself capable of constructing an exact model of the universe. But now things have fundamentally changed, so much so that we are profoundly frightened at the uncertainty and time-bound mutability of human views. An entirely new and subtle world presents itself to our dazed minds, a world in which there is no longer any standard of absolute value, a world in which time no longer governs independently, but is locked together with space into a four-dimensional continuum, a world in which every insect possesses a "world-line," in which electrons race around protons with calculable velocity even though neither the former nor the latter exists except hypothetically. The non-mathematical mind believes itself transported back to the centuries of gnosticism when it reads of the purely symbolic nature of physical quantities, of the loose, reduced causality of the material universe, of the hail of quanta, and of such things as radiation-gradient.

James Jeans writes in his book, *The Universe Around Us,* about the Creation of Matter, - "All this makes it clear that the present matter of the universe cannot have existed forever: indeed we can probably assign an upper limit to its age of, say, some such round number as 200 million million years. And, wherever we fix it, our next step back in time leads us to contemplate a definite event, or series of events, or continuous process, of creation of matter at some time not infinitely remote. In some way matter which had not previously existed, came, or was brought, into being.—If we want a naturalistic interpretation of this creation of matter, we may imagine radiant energy of any wavelength less than 1.3 x 10^{-13} cms. being poured into empty space; this is energy of higher 'availability' than any known in the present universe, and the running down of such energy might well create a universe similar to our own."

The radiant energy of "higher availability" about which our modern scientist speaks singularly coincides with the "*pneuma*" of the Ophites and the Basilides, which emanates from the Logos and sinks down through the region of the fixed stars and planets, becoming more and more dense. This coincidence is doubtless no accident. It indicates that the temporal state of consciousness to which the entire spiritual life of our age is subject, namely, naturalistic nihilism, is approaching its break-up, and that the science of matter, without even being aware of it, is entering in mathematical guise into the sphere of irrational speculation. The analogy of the early-Christian, late-classical era with the present age has already been frequently emphasized by modern historians. Apparently we can hear the soft overtones of a new sympathetic note.

Matter, not as a philosophic abstract but as a solid object of physical research, evaporates into something thought of, indeed, into something inconceivable except as a mathematical fiction. Little as all this has to do with mysticism, it nonetheless appears that, after a long time, once again there is a rent in the curtain of knowledge through which streams the spiritual sun of transcendency. However, since I am neither qualified nor capable of presuming to express an opinion about science, I shall let two great physicists speak, English professors, world-famed scholars who are marching in the vanguard of the new system of knowledge.

One of them, Eddington, attests that, "The idea of a universal Mind or Logos would be, I think, a fairly plausible inference from the present state of scientific theory; at least it is in harmony with it." (*The Nature of the Physical World*, p. 338.)

And James Jeans, the other scientist, judges that, "Modern scientific theory compels us to think of the Creator as working outside time and space, which are part of His creation, just as the artist is outside his canvas. It acords with the conjecture of Augustine: '*Non in tempore, sed cum tempore, finxit Deus mundum.*'" (*The Mysterious Universe*, Revised Edition, p. 182.)

We are well aware of the fact that these quotations represent opinions of physicists and not principles of physics. Yet, could anything indicate the revolution of science more clearly than these general views of physical scientists?

For the time being, this is still a feeble admission, no more than an embarrassed recognition of transcendency as a plausible inference. And yet, thirty years ago a physicist would probably have considered it scientifically compromising to break the naturalistic obligation of maintaining dead silence concerning God. However that may be, old and honorable matter has lost its solid foundation. The alert understanding can no longer sit back complacently in the secure atmosphere of foregone conclusions. The atom has expanded into a minutely vast solar system with its space an almost complete vacuum; visible, palpable matter has contracted from a solid, motionless, compact mass of extremely minute particles into a magical structure of curves of inconceivable motion and radiation. Thus the occult becomes clear as day and the day's clearness becomes occult. Scientific knowledge is not absolute truth, but consists of more or less logically ascertained forms of interpretation by means of which the historically-conditioned consciousness attempts to explain certain observations and experiments. The manner in which the view of the objective world is changing reveals primarily the direction in which the consciousness of our time is tending to develop. In spite of strict mathematical method the step from classical mechanics to the new speculative physics (at least in the mystic content of its ideas) signifies a step from the rational towards the irrational. A process once begun must continue to its conclusion. Let us be patient. Perhaps it will be a physicist who will one day unwittingly let a higher Personality enter the world through some absolutely forbidden portal.

VII

Religion would be in a bad way if it had need of the theistic midwife services of science. "The nearest road to God is through the gate of love. The road of science is slow indeed to Him," said Angelus Silesius. Religion remains steadfast within its own truths. And among its objective, historical truths belong the revelations and inspired doctrines of the salvation of humanity. Concerning these I shall remain reverently silent, as I promised at the beginning of this essay.

Permit me to make only one brief observation. Modern geologists teach that man, whose historical memory embraces less than ten thousand years, may be several hundred thousand years old. In all probability, on the other hand, a few billion centuries still lie before him. Consequently, man is at the present time at the very beginning of his primitive history. Let us imagine that there is an aerial cableway leading from the earth to the moon, - and let its length symbolize humanity's entire course of history from its recent beginning to its remote end, - then we have advanced scarcely one centimeter along this cableway. During this ridiculously short stretch of the way, however, divinely inspired men have constantly arisen and have borne bloody witness to the certainty of a divine over-world. They were the supremely great spirits and characters who lived among mortals. And we who now occupy the thousandth part of a millimeter along this way, a part that calls itself enlightened, we presume to be superior to these exalted founders because we have learned to toss about vacuous and artful words like "pathological," "auto-suggestion," and the like. (At this point it would be appropriate to refer to the so-called *"Theodicee ex consensu gentium,"* to the historical proof of God, which is based upon the fact that an inner perception of Divinity is unanimously confirmed by all peoples, even by those who were unaware of each other's existence.)

We consider the revelation of truth by those divinely inspired men as childish fantasy, because of all instruments of knowledge, we have developed in recent times only that of logic, and we think we can outsmart the mystery of the universe by the one and only *"more geometrico."* The mystery smiles, for in the last analysis every language of formulas proves nothing but its own presuppositions. Have we reached our goal? Is it not possible that we shall still experience miracles along this same millimeter of our journey through the universe?

No philosopher has yet succeeded in separating consciousness from reality within his philosophical system. The material world is just as much a part of my consciousness as is the idea of God. As children we grow aware of the one as well as of the other through organic heritage and through instruction. If the heritage is tainted, if the instruction falls short, the result is an idiot, whether it be with regard to reality or with regard to the idea of God.

I shall also remain silent regarding the two fundamental facts of subjective religious experience, that is, prayer and grace, since any consideration of these belongs to the realm of theology. Probably all people are familiar with prayer but only few with grace. However, I should like to confine myself to a phenomenon which is accessible and which lies beyond actual piety. Let us call it religious experience.

This profoundest of human experiences includes ten thousand degrees and stages, beginning with the simplest rapture at nature's wonder to the saint's *unio mystica* with God. It is based upon the intuitive apprehension of a supersensual counter-image in the sense-clouded mirror of our consciousness. If in the melting instant of sexual love, *You* and *I* are obliterated and death grows remote, in religious ecstasy death is not only remote but is inconsequential; there is no death. And the human *I* is not obliterated but is sublimated, and that in the threefold, profound connotation of the word: Sublimated =Dissolved=Refined=Exalted. Here language ends, or better, it shies like a spirited steed. It is scarcely possible to describe musical experience in words. Technical terms like *tonic, dominant* and *cadence* do not convey any melody. But it is absolutely impossible to convey through language the deepest of all spiritual experiences.

Plato avows that "On this subject I have never written anything and never will; for it is not expressible in words like other subjects of instruction; but if one has lived with it long enough, it suddenly rises up in the soul like a light ignited by a flickering fire, and then continues to feed itself by its own strength." (Epistle VII, 341)

And another philosopher tells us that "The ecstatic state can never be adequately described in words. - God, too, is unnameable, inexpressible, exalted beyond all speech: the 'abyss,' silence. *Atman* is also called 'the Silent One.' " (From Friedrich Heiler's *Prayer,* a study in the history and philosophy of religion, Munich, 1918.)

A philosopher once made the brilliant remark that there are people who are religiously unmusical. By that he meant people who are affected by religious experience as little as some are affected by music. I deny that there are people who are really unreligious (beyond a minute number of exceptions), as I have already denied that there are people hopelessly untouched by the spirit of the muses. The truth is that, for many reasons, the fundamental values of life have not been uncovered or else have been buried in millions of humans.

What can each individual do to uncover these values? The answer is simple. Let him first of all realize how monstrously we are, all of us, wasting our precious time. Let him salvage one hour of solitude from the ruins of his day. This will be the hour to take up the struggle consciously against the demons of the cares of life, of ulterior thoughts, of vain dreams of power and success, in order to penetrate to our inner Self where the decision lies.

Into the dense darkness of our very first meeting with our Self shines the premonition of eternal light. The more man humbles himself before it, the more disdainfully will he shut his ears to the vulgar call of base allurements. The more unconditionally he surrenders to this eternal light, the freer will he remain in the world of reality when the raucous command of party politics summons him to action. The more he is at home in the great Question, the stranger will he feel in the world of the platitudinous Answer. Consciousness is transformed, and only in that lies renewal.

If we view all the revolutionary and reform movements in the spiritual sphere within the last decade, but particularly the radical works of literature, we undoubtedly come to the conclusion that these supposed feats of liberation are nothing else than the passionate attempt to safeguard and dam off against metaphysical danger the constitution of the time-spirit and nihilism's general state of consciousness. The agitators of boundless psychology, of radical literature, of the sexual question and so forth, reveal themselves to the astute gaze as strict conservatives, defending with grim fury intellectualism and its broader implications. These agitators run along in the worn-out ruts of borrowed values, and their intoxication with progress is only an intoxication induced by the speed at which they whiz from one point in the void to the other. But today, the true warrior of freedom can only be the one who leaps out of this rut.

118

Only the uncontrollable longing for the charismatic profundities of life can vouchsafe to us the power to destroy the nihilism within us.

Everyone to whom it is granted to awake out of the practical soddenness of mere vegetative existence can become a servant in the renewal of the general consciousness. Only one thing is demanded of him, that he decide for or against the Divine, and that he should not evade the central question of existence. If he has hitherto been of the opinion that an "assumptionless" science has done away with God, and that, as a believer in God, he puts himself into the ranks of reactionary fools, let him now take mental account of the true state of affairs: science, to be sure, cannot prove the existence of God, but even less can it disprove His existence, a fact that the greatest and most honest minds of science have always acknowledged and professed. The Divine is a tender music of the innermost soul; it is something which can be, but need not necessarily be, perceived. In order to detect it, it is indispensable that the spiritual ear be turned to it, that there be a decision, an act of will. Doubt is the first stirring of this will, and hence doubt is of infinitely greater stature than indifference, which is only an expression of grossly inferior, spiritual plebeianism. Behind this indifference nihilism entrenches itself most firmly; for by doubting, man extends his little finger to God and thus incurs the danger of having his entire hand seized.

By directing our attention upon the inner perception of the Divine, we have taken the first step towards conquering the modern state of consciousness. Before anything else stands the admonition: "Knock and it shall be opened unto you." More cannot be said. And even that which could or can be said pursues the single goal of making the secure insecure, and the insecure secure, wherein by "secure" is meant those who are secure in their skepticism, and by "insecure" those who are insecure in their faith.

VIII

The world of nihilism! We dare not forget that most European races, the Germans, Celts, and Slavs, have only been Christianized not much more than a thousand years. Since the Renaissance, approximately, they have been experiencing a grave relapse into heathenism. Nihilism with its political *Ersatz*-religions is the last phase of this relapse.

It is especially as a Jew, by virtue of a primeval affinity of blood and character, that I feel myself justified in the following view: this world that calls itself civilized can be spiritually healed only if it finds its way back to true Christianity. "Why?" ask the sacristans of agnosticism and atheism. Because the teaching of Christ, - so the deeper insight must confess, - not only is not exhausted but has scarcely been felt. Because in its metaphysical and ethical values, it towers star-high above every trend of the present day. Because it places the gross, materialistic barbarian, the stockholder of nothingness, and the possessed possessor of personal interests in Europe and its environs before the sacred paradox, "Live contrary to your interests for Truth and Life!"

But even with respect to worldly matters we must recognize that man's salvation can never issue forth out of philosophical systems, theosophical groups, sects and schismatic religions, but only out of a general, world-embracing, i.e. catholic frame of faith.

It cannot be denied that even our nihilistic time favors us with all sorts of unctuous little maxims, "Be good, be honest, do no evil, think of your fellow man, don't shirk responsibility, etc."

To the devil with such tripe! Why should I be good and honest and not do evil and not shirk responsibility? I am only a whirl of some idiotic electrons which paste together a bit of muck, electrons which in a short time will fly apart, not without a stench. There will be no trace of me in the world-process. So it's all the same whether I do evil or good, which, incidentally, are only two anthropomorphic concepts. If responsibility is to have meaning, then eternal consequences must follow from my actions. But what does follow from my actions is null and void. My feeling of responsibility merely subjects me uncritically to the exploitive purposes of society, be it capitalistic or socialistic. Morality is, in my opinion, only the art of gaining my own ends without becoming a criminal. Well, what do you say? For whom shall I sacrifice myself? For the next generation? For my children? And how do you justify, if I may ask, this queasy, sentimentally humanitarian lie? I am living here and now. The chance will not come again. I will not give it up for anyone. That business of the future and the children is empty metaphysics, hypocritically dished out by the entire clergy, from the Catholic to the Marxist. I won't be made a fool of! Since nothing has any meaning, the struggle for the satisfaction of my urges is the sole reality.

Thus, in truth, would every ethic be which did not rest in divine affinity.* If such an ethic is not as vehement as the Iago-like confession above, it is due to convention and inertia, to the family and herd instinct of the human animal.

Only when we are assured of an eternal perfection do we grow aware of our own imperfection. Only when we are convinced of the eternal continuance of the temporal moment does life appear capable of direction. Thus originates the feeling of guilt, our most sacred feeling without which there can be no refinement and progress. Through the telescope of the feeling of guilt we divine the unattainable above us and become worthy of the longing to share in it. We enter the status of reverence. But reverence transforms all that is earthly, especially one's relationship to others. Only reverence can transform the social and national community of interests into a true and general brotherliness, just as it transforms sexuality into love. And love transforms marriage. And the transformed marriage transforms the begetting

---

* In this sense even that icy rationalist, Kant, found himself obliged to construct a "moral proof of the existence of God." - "We must assume a moral World-Cause (an Author of the World) in order to set before ourselves a final purpose in accordance with the moral law; and in so far as the latter is necessary, so far (i.e. in the same degree and for the same reason) must the former also be necessarily assumed; i.e. we must assume that there is a God." - "........ or should he (the well-meaning individual) in this matter also desire to remain loyal to the call of his inner moral destiny and not to weaken his sense of awe (with which the moral law directly inspires him to obedience) by the *nullity* of a single, ideal *final purpose* appropriate to its exalted demand, which cannot happen without harm befalling his moral outlook,—then he must make an assumption, which, indeed, he can very well do because it is in itself not contradictory in practical intent; i.e. in order at least to conceive the notion of the possibility of the final purpose prescribed for him, he must assume the the existence of a moral *Author of the World,* i.e. of a God." (Dialectic of the Teleological Judgement, §87.)

The language of "practical reason" seems to be twisting like a serpent before the Author of the World.

of children. The latter is no longer a disagreeable accident between two acts of contraception. The transformed begetting of children transforms the value of the children. So one transformation flows out of the other until death, which is the final transformation. Since death no longer means a transition into Nothing but a transition into Something, it loses its terror. And when death loses its terror then life loses its brutal grimness. In our soul blossoms the tender irony of art and of play, for at the basis of play lies the feeling of continuity and of security, the feeling that we are children of God.

If any of my readers should see only an unreal daydream in this chain of transformations, my efforts will have been in vain. I take my chain of causes just as seriously as communists take their classless society; indeed, I venture to assert that a just, human order can only be formed as I have indicated. Only I should like to set the date for the salvation of humanity more cautiously than do the political doctrines of faith.

The road is clear. It begins here, directly before us. And a very troublesome road it is. It demands work, study, criticism, struggle, solitude, pangs of conscience, decision and renunciation. The void still clings to us all with a thousand tentacles. It is inconceivably difficult to convert oneself to divine affinity out of nihilistic non-affinity and in the face of temporal opinion. But we must hope that the procedure will be of benefit to us. All who are in despair should set forth upon this road. Its goal is the goal of all the world: Joy.

A Summary
of Some Principal Reasons Why Faith in God Appears Necessary and Unavoidable

First:

THE INNER PERCEPTION OF THE DIVINE

(The Psychological Reason)

The inner perception of the Divine is attested to in thousands of documents, from the beginning of history down to our day. The manner in which a given historical state of consciousness interprets such spiritual experience constitutes no argument against the existence of what this experience is based upon. Though the anti-God philosophy of religion may psychologically disintegrate these interpretations and their results (cults, rites, dogmas), it cannot dissolve their intrinsic content of feeling. The foundation of this content remains unimpaired, however its surface may appear in the light of day. The reason why this content of feeling so seldom enters the consciousness lies in the fact that an imageless, extra-sensory mode of experience is inexpressible in speech. Therefore, even in thought it can be visualized only under quite extraordinary circumstances.

In view of this, the strongest argument against any atheistic philosophy of history, lies in the fact that it invariably and manifestly reveals the endeavor to demonstrate *a posteriori* its embittered premise that there is no God. Accordingly, it is not a science but an emotional intent.

Second:

MAN ASCRIBES MEANING TO THE WORLD

(The Logical Reason)

Our spiritual existence operates as an inexhaustible process of ascribing meanings which we strew over all things. As intellectual beings we can as little conceive meaninglessness as a square circle or a bent straight line. Without an over-meaning, i.e. without world-conception, world-creation, world-direction, the universe would be meaningless and therefore inconceivable; for the assumption of a partial-meaning, by the very nature of thought, involves the certainty of a universal meaning and of an eternally-caused interrelationship. This is an attitude of our mental character as naive as it is unchangeable, an attitude which no artificiality of logic or of the theory of knowledge can in any way change.

Without meaning and logical consistency, therefore, nothing is conceivable, for thinking itself is based on the acknowledgment of meaning and consistency. However, in acknowledging meaning and consistency we posit (since indeed the chain of inferences cannot be broken at will) a first and last meaning, and an eternal logical consistency which is God.

Accordingly, if we look at the external world and take thoughtful (symbolic and consistent) account of its phenomena, then God is the first and last premise of this account, regardless whether we confess Him or not.

Third:

MAN ASCRIBES VALUE TO THE WORLD
(The Moral Reason)

Naturalistic nihilism defines human morality as the renunciation of impulse, a renunciation imposed upon the individual by the demands of the general welfare. The commandment "Thou shalt not kill" thus receives the following supplement: "because it is not advantageous to society and hence, indirectly, not advantageous to yourself." This conception acknowledges only two impulses in the soul; indeed, it considers the soul synonymous with these two impulses: the impulse of desire and the impulse of aggressiveness. The non-ego, fellow man and creature, shrinks into a mere object of exploitation of desire and destruction, culture shrinks into domesticated crime. The doctrine of murder-lust and of lust-murder as the ultimate end of the soul is by no means an exaggeration but the legitimate psychological inference of the nihilistic attitude of our era. To this attitude, the good denotes merely an evil frustrated for the purpose of a general possibility of life.

Were this insight not only a somber conclusion of despair but the unveiling of the real state of affairs, its propagation would have to be forbidden as a mortal danger. For it leaves only two ways open to the man who follows them to their ultimate conclusion: suicide or crime; suicide, because it is unbearably degrading to vegetate in an inferno whose life-basis is formed by an inescapable although neutralized cannibalism; crime

127

because it is no less degrading to eke out one's existence in a world entirely devoid of meaning, reason and consistency, without daring to enjoy to the full the only reality that has a convincing meaning, the satisfaction of desire. Seen in such sharp focus, man's creation and the creation of organic matter in general—(it feeds upon itself as one creature murders another)—is undoubtedly a crime. Accordingly, there is no absolute, adequate ground why the individual human being, who is the fruit of a crime, should not be a criminal.

Though this train of reasoning may seem grossly over-simplified, no purely naturalistic theory of morals can surmount the dilemma that it poses. The pretended collective advantage is not a high enough value to justify the individual's abstention in the long run; humanity as a consumers' union and insurance company denotes no ideal that could ever sway even a single young person once he recognized its hopeless inanity. Life as a kind of cosmic shipwreck and the spirit as the emergency consequence of this shipwreck, such a philosophy of history is not a *Weltanschauung* but only a diseased, bilious mood of the time-spirit originating from the empty or upset stomach of the present.

There can neither be, nor is there, any other morality within naturalistic nihilism. Its complete impotence constitutes its chief characteristic, whereby it strikingly proves that it is not a morality at all. Insofar as the human spirit has not already become indifferent, that is, unspiritual, nihilistic morality, with logical necessity, plunges it into a salvationless abyss of pessimism and the sadness of futility. When this morality dispenses its bitterness to us in sugared concepts as "energy" or "progress," it commits, as we already know, the dishonesty of borrowing from metaphysics terms to be used against metaphysics.

Fortunately, however, it can never conquer the spirit even though it temporarily casts a pall over it. The reason for this lies not alone in the sensual trammels of our nature which, after all, endures life and goes about its business under the worst practical and philosophical conditions. For just as the human mind can experience the external world only apperceptively, i.e. cognitively, by constantly giving it meaning, so also, it is only by constantly giving the world values that the mind can actively enter into relationship with it. Ascribing meanings as well as ascribing values is a naive attitude of the human mind and, as has already been said, wholly independent of epistemological speculations concerning their possibility or impossibility. But they are also no less independent of genetic psychology which, to be sure, can describe the evolutionary process and manner of reaction of a phenomenon but cannot interpret its essence. (The fact that a rose originates out of an insignificant seed is no argument against its beauty and fragrance.) Hence, as thought is based on acknowledgment of meaning, so conduct is based on acknowledgment of value. From the very nature of cognition a meaningless world is unthinkable; and, by the same token, neither is a valueless world experienceable.

The next step in this analogy introduces a difficulty. We have said of thought, "If we acknowledge meaning and logical consistency, we necessarily posit a first and ultimate meaning and an eternal logical consistency which is God. For it is in the nature of thought that it cannot voluntarily stop drawing logical conclusions."

Against the analogous sentence, "If we acknowledge value we necessarily posit a first and ultimate value, a supreme good, i.e. God," naturalism will object, "Our valuation is determined by desire and non-desire." Very well. But modern psychology teaches that every individual has learned to curtail his desire-determined valuations in favor of a collective good. Now where does this collective good begin and where does it end? Family, clan, race, nation, mankind, creatures? The individual makes his impulse-sacrifices according to his spiritual scope. A loving mother dies for her children. That, at any rate, can still be interpreted as extended egoism. But, for what extended egoism or collective advantage did Jesus Christ die? Was it perhaps for the temporal welfare of Juda? Did Socrates, perhaps, drink the cup of hemlock for the prosperity and future of the Athens that he knew so well? And all the saints and martyrs who have suffered a bloody and fiery death? No! Everyone of these deaths was directed against the empirical world and society. It is quite apparent that the positing of values in its highest form as self-sacrifice can just as little stop with a definite, utility-conditioned collective as thought's innate ascription of meaning can stop at a given link in the chain of logic. Thought and valuation are equally inexhaustible intentions directed towards the infinite. Functionally inherent in both is the logical advance from the smaller to the greater, from the special to the general. The relation in logical inference between the particular and the universal is known. The process of ascribing values operates similarly. Should a true moralist, for example, limit himself to seeing ultimate value in his kindred or in his nation, a value for which all abstention from impulse is to be exercised? No! For if he limits himself so soon, he merely demonstrates that he possesses an inadequate morality. One is not a good human being if one is only a good Frenchman or a good German. One is not even a good human being if one is only a good human being. Love (all-embracing sympathy) pervades all creatures by virtue of its innate development from the smaller to the greater. Nor does love stop at the universe, at the sensual world; in the greatest individuals it is exalted into love of the over-world, the supernatural, into love of God. That is the mystery of the *Passion,* of the sacrificial death which is suffered for the sake of the Creator no less than for the sake of creatures.

Analytic psychology has coined the splendid word "sublimation" for the mechanism by means of which moral values develop from the lower to the higher, from the ego to the universe. By this technical term, however, psychology admits the existence of that striving for development which, in opposition to egostistical gratification, sacrifices a lesser value in order to gain a higher one. Since psychology, in acknowledging this mechanism, must simultaneously admit the advance from the lower to the higher (e.g. sublimation of gregariousness into nationalism), there would remain only one thing for it to do in order to surmount the naturalistic barrier; namely, that it should admit the unsatisfiable and infinite tendency of the phenomenon of sublimation.

Paradoxically expressed: whoever does not devour a defenseless enemy thereby has already, without knowing it, affirmed the existence of God. Why? Because he has abstained from his own cannibalistic satisfaction for the sake of the life of a next higher unity. Thereby however, he is already entering upon the road leading from the individual to the universal and therefore to the infinite and to God. Upon this road he will continue to walk according to the measure of his will and of his strength. Whoever does not deny that the community is a value superior to the individual, must, if he can think and feel logically, recognize that one circle of the community is concentrically surrounded by the next and that he is confined within all these circles. Logically there is no possibility for him to hide in the innermost circle,—the outermost circle still encloses him. If in connection with the whole, he takes his first-nearest step towards the good (no matter how this step may psychologically appear conditioned by advantage), he is already, by this small step, affirming the last-farthest goal of sublimation or the supreme, all-encompassing good. Without this supreme good the first step could not even be taken; for, as in a world without meaning there would be no thought, so in a world without value there would be no sublimation.

In other words, a naturalistic morality which is only based on the definition of abstention from impulse in favor of some majority and not upon the consciousness of infinite valuation and with it the certainty of God, does not exist and cannot exist.

Fourth:

IF TRUTH CANNOT, THEN BEAUTY DECIDES

(The Esthetic Reason)

Science possesses no means of proving the existence of the Divine. But neither has it any means, as we have shown, of denying it. Science, consequently, is forced by its orientation to declare as an illusion the hypothesis of a God-pervaded world as well as of a godless world.

From mathematics we know that, of two correct solutions to a problem, that one must be preferred which achieves the result in the shorter, simpler and hence more beautiful way. And by this token, when truth no longer has anything to say, the decision as to the value of a mental process is entrusted to beauty.

This is a marvelous indication of what our attitude must be in the face of two modes of contemplation the truth of which cannot be demonstrated with logical and verbal means, and which because of their missing and hence equivalent results, play a role similar to the two solutions of the mathematical problem. Since science resigns in the face of ultimate things, whereas we, on the other hand, as spiritual beings cannot live without a philosophy (which, after all, can be nothing else than a creed concerning ultimate things), we are empowered to make a decision between these two non-solutions or illusions. Consequently, even if we should adopt the standpoint of coldest agnosticism and should assume that

133

the conclusions concerning the true and the good do not rightly belong in the problem of metaphysics, we nevertheless may unhesitatingly submit to the judgment of beauty by weighing against each other the *esthetic values* of a God-pervaded and of a godless world.

We have a choice between two worlds. One has no meaning and no value, for value and meaning are merely anthropomorphisms and arbitrary teleology which we do not derive from this world but merely attribute to it. Even though we are capable of hypothetically deducing a few laws in regard to matter (which on the morrow turn out to be errors), the ultimate purpose of organic and inorganic nature still remains eternally closed to us; indeed, the very assumption of an ultimate purpose is a logically prohibited presumption. Regarding ourselves, the human race, we have a smattering of history and psychology. Both show us that it is the economic principle primarily that motivates all development. This economic principle corresponds to the principle of "adaptation" and the "struggle for existence" formulated by Darwin. Since primitive man had no claws, talons, horns, tusks and similar weapons, he was forced to develop his intelligence as a weapon. All spiritual accomplishments, therefore, all doctrines of salvation, philosophies, works of art, Plato's Dialogues and the Ninth Symphony originate out of the precarious accident that a rather cunning species of baboon possessed no other physical weapon than his intellect. It is the mission of this parvenu species of baboon in the course of time to subjugate the natural forces of the earth in order to assure the mastery of his own species against all cosmic and tellurian adversities and against all social inconveniences, and in order to grant to the individual a just measure of welfare (such is the only and highest naturalistic ideal of the future). That completes the story, unless we add that man was undoubtedly born only in order to decay. On this road from nothing to nothing, however, the brief interruption which is life is revealed as a highly superfluous disturbance of placid non-existence. Hence, indifference is the only philosophy that can be logically justified, just as painlessness is the only real good that is to be striven for.*

This is one of the solutions or non-solutions, that presents itself as a choice. It might also be entitled "the illusion of disillusionment."

In contrast to this, the other world is primarily distinguished by the fact that it is a world of meaning and value. Whoever professes it, is of the conviction that man as a part of the whole cannot possess anything that the whole does not possess. If then, as a splinter of the cosmos, the tendency towards ascribing meaning and value is inherent in him, this tendency can be only a pale reflection, a feeble counterpart, of those qualities of meaning and value that lie within the universe itself. Whoever believes in the meaning and value of the universe, at the same time believes in its spiritual content; he believes that creation is a spiritual act. Within the belief in this act of creation is co-contained the belief in the power of creation which must represent the highest principle of the quality of meaning (spirit) and the quality of value (love). Consequently, the necessary

---

* This conclusion is drawn by the almost atheistic, or at least atheological, doctrine of Buddhism, which actually raises the destruction of suffering to the supreme good.

result for anyone who acknowledges meaning and value in the world is faith in the Deity, who is Supreme Spirit and Foremost Love. (Dante: *La somma sapienza e il primo amore*). On the contrary, however, the denial of God entails the denial of even the slightest meaning and value in the world. Faith radically changes man's attitude towards life. Whereas to the godless man the history of the development of the human mind is striking evidence of its matter-born limitations, to the believer the genetic sciences prove nothing but the fact that the entelechy of the spirit and of love in man must go through certain stages as must everything created into organic nature. The believer is not a historical man but a man of the everlasting present. Whereas the world realist sees in morality only a purposive attitude that has as its ultimate goal the life-security and satisfaction of the human race's wants (castaways on a desert isle), the man imbued with a sense of the Divine recognizes his mission in the realization of spirit and love, in the deification of man, far beyond this human compromise of the "struggle for existence" and "adaptation." Whereas the one announces "welfare for all" the other proclaims "happiness and joy for all." The skeptic finds only the external world in his inner world, i.e. a world without meaning and value. Consequently, he turns away from his inner world because its emptiness is more painful than the emptiness of the factual world which at least is relieved by noise and hubbub. As a harried exile of his ego he plunges into a sea of activity whereby he creates false wants in social life and causes a great deal of harm. The believer finds the external world in his inner world as well, but it has meaning and value. However, he finds in himself something else besides this external world, namely, the experience of the supersensual significance of all sensual phenomena. Within his soul he grows aware of a focal point that gathers all the rays of spirit and of love; it is the focus of the inner perception of the Divine. For him, the inner world is richer than the sensual world and, according to the law of advancement from the smaller to the greater, from the special to the general, he turns his gaze within. He shuns activity and loves contemplation. The inner contemplation also reveals to him those other values and powers that revolve like planets around the central sun of religious experience, the muse-like, creative forces of the soul. He suddenly comprehends enthusiasm as the supreme potential of life; and the view of religion that the angels' purpose of existence is an eternal paean, the uninterrupted "sanctus-sanctus-sanctus," no longer appears meaningless to him. When he arises out of his depression he is richer than before and his full heart desires to communicate itself to others. Thereby he makes people richer, in contrast to the busy-body who drives them along in the harried chase after nothing, and who exploits and robs them.

The skeptic believes in nothing *more* than in death; the believer believes in nothing *less*. Since the world is to him a creation of spirit and love, he cannot be threatened by eternal destruction in his essential being as a creature of the world, since indeed, not even the matter of which he is composed is destroyed, but merely enters into new combinations. The most important personality-building element of his small, human mind is the organ of mental relationship, memory. The believer believes that God created man in His own image. Nihilism inverts the sentence and says that man has created God in his own image. But we already know that this is a homology. Man cannot bring forth anything that has not been put into him. Without the inner perception of the Divine, he would never have been able to interpret the latter.

Accordingly, corresponding to the human memory, there must be an infinitely more precise and more perfect universal memory of the Deity. No one can comprehend its nature. But one thing is sure: whatever condition may prevail beyond space and time, not a breath of living and lived life can disappear from it. That is why the believer believes less in death than he does in anything else.

We have thus briefly portrayed the two worlds open to our choice. Philosophically, the truth and reality of neither of these worlds is demonstrable. Before the tribunal of logic they are only disillusioned and illusory illusions. Hence, they are equally justifiable in this perspective. The strict example of mathematics permits us to set up beauty as an arbiter so that she may pass judgment where truth has no more to say. The question is, "Which of these two worlds is the more beautiful, that is, more harmonious, more heart-quickening, more full of the promise of happiness, more conducive to satisfaction, richer?" The very question suggests the answer.

We have here undertaken the forbidden attempt of transferring the problem of faith in God out of the realm of religion into the field of general human contemplation. Those whose outlook is strictly scientific will miss the cogent conclusiveness that they demand of their deductions. Those who are strict in their faith will miss the reference to the dogmatic structure of the particular religion in which they see everything ordered and affirmed for all eternity. Some may find fault with the idea that esthetics, the principle of beauty, was invoked in order to decide between the God-pervaded and godless worlds, as between two glasses of equally good wine. There's no quarreling about taste. Incidentally, the phrase is wrong. If there is no quarreling about the object of taste, there can and certainly must be quarreling about the subject of taste. Taste is nothing but a person's capacity for differentiating and evaluating. Whoever knows how to differentiate more sharply and to evaluate more intolerantly than another has more taste than this other. In accord with these arguments there can be no further doubt that the choice of the God-pervaded world presupposes a more differentiated mind, a mind more imbued with value and touched by the muses, than the choice of the godless world. A glance not only into history but into our immediate environment shows us that it is much rather the fine, differentiated and higher individual and not the vulgar one who inclines towards belief in a spiritual and godly world. It is an insolent lie which contends that atheism is a mark of the intellectual aristocrat whereas faith is the dull, spiritual pabulum of the proletarian. The exact opposite is true.

Now, to be sure, at the present time there is a remarkable cowardice prevalent among intellectuals that keeps many from looking the greatest question of life straight in the eye. We have repeatedly expatiated upon the reasons for this cowardice. To the false belief that true science claims the decision is added an unconscious confusion of the idea of God not only with the hierarchy, but with its political caricature that has been dinned into our souls by the centuries of enlightenment and liberalism. Ridiculous as it may sound, the name of God and the thought of a spiritual over-world arouses in many intelligent and wide-awake people the terrible associations of the Dark Ages, the Inquisition, the torture chamber, Galileo, and pogroms! An absurd, fairy-tale belief!—There are great problems here for a psychology of nations, classes, and generations. Before analytic psychology uses its knife to dissect the human concept of God, it should in all honesty examine the dark lust for revenge that whets the knife.

It is high time for the spiritually awake individual to acknowledge, "I dare not shirk the ultimate question without remaining a craven weakling on earth, having no firm foundation. All my individual views and special accomplishments do not help me to achieve a real philosophy. Though I may be considered intelligent, I am at best only an astute but wavering shadow." Whoever sees this clearly with the full painfulness of realization, can no longer be satisfied with the spiritual substitutes with which the present provides him in a hundred forms; he will finally begin to doubt that which is the only thing to be doubted. And once he has lost his empty, naturalistic *Ersatz*-faith, he will be permitted to penetrate to his innermost self, that is, to the perception of the Divine which is waiting for him to hearken unto it.

Then it will take him by the hand and disclose to him step by step the miracle of an everyday world into which the over-world extends, and the miracle of this over-world which is pervaded by the everyday world.

Theologoumena

A PRIMER FOR AGNOSTICS

1

Liber Scriptus Proferetur
In Quo Totum Continetur

I am a letter of the alphabet somewhere in a huge, thick novel. I don't know my own meaning nor the meaning of the few neighboring letters that I can see from where I am. I don't know what syllable we belong to that, together with other syllables, composes the unknown word that includes us and that, together with countless oher unknown words, forms the lines that neatly fill the pages of the book. Since I do not even know the why and wherefore of the letter that I myself am, how could I know anything about the meaning of the entire, huge, thick novel, about its plot, its arrangement, about its structure, its beginning and end, its complications and dénouements, its main and minor characters, - to say nothing about its author? But since I am nevertheless one letter of the great whole, holding hands as in a mysterious round dance, with adjacent letters incomprehensible to me; and since, consequently, I am situated in a connected whole, in the continuous flow of the narrative inscrutable to me yet also pervading my own existence, I am filled with the steadfast consciousness of being a meaningful particle that is easily deciphered and related to other particles by the eyes of someone beyond the book who is reading or writing me. Irradiated by those eyes beyond, the tiny letter cherishes the secure hope, nay, the proud presentiment that it is not only necessary to the whole for its totality but also contains within its own minuteness the utterly unknown meaning of that whole.

2

ON THAT WHICH IS PERMITTED TO MAN

Only in very small measure are men permitted on earth to use the cosmic forces for the greedy exigencies of their welfare and their hate: steam, magnetism, electricity, long and short waves, that is about all. It seems as though a weakened and weary Deity were letting us toy a little with His lightning, but only quite superficially and childishly. The Deity has seen to it that we should not be able to create any real mischief in the universe in spite of all our proud technology and in spite of all our theoretical splitting of the atom. We are not even permitted to scratch the crust of our tiny planet nor to penetrate into the depths of our dwelling place.

3

God permits nature to grant us humans the ability of killing each other. This permission proves to us that death is not real, nor conclusive; nor is it genuine state of non-existence; for otherwise killing would be as little a matter of choice for creatures as the above-mentioned grave misuse of cosmic forces.

Thus evil, too, is placed into our mischievous hands only as a kind of plaything which in time reveals our own worthiness or unworthiness without being able to cause any serious damage.

ON THE MYSTERY OF INCARNATION

1

Why is the word of God (the Son) more than the works of God (creatures)? Because, of all making and doing (*poiein*), word-working (*poiesis,* poesy) is the deed most spiritual and most real.

2

The word that issues forth from the mouth is closer to the existence of the Creator than any work of the hands. Therein lies the preeminence of the Son and the preeminence of poesy.

3

In order properly to approach the mystery of incarnation, one must not only conceive it in its social and creature aspects, that is, in its love function. Far beyond that, it is an intra-personal act within the Deity, having nothing to do with creation.

4

The analogous word "Life," applied to the Deity, as in the expression "Living God," is the most delicate of all analogies. We cannot represent life other than as "pulses in time," or, to coin a verb, "time-functioning" (*"zeiten"*). This "time-functioning," however, is in complete contrast to the life of the Deity, which is most profoundly humiliated by its representation as a pulse-beat, that is, as a motion which is destined to end.

5

MOTTO FOR PEACEMAKERS
Not revenge, but expiation!
Not punishment, but penance!

6

Only the eternally most changeable can hope to meet the eternally most unchangeable. This is why every petrified religion is like a blasphemy.

7

The second person is the social aspect in the Deity. *Verbum caro factum.* This not only applies to the Son but, in another sense, to the world also. All created things are expressed words. The Son is that essence of God which does not contemplate itself, like the Father, but has to do exclusively with the world, as the first and uncreated and yet incarnate Word above all words.

8

Only the Son can transsupplicate the Father's self-contemplation into world-contemplation. That is the meaning of Jesus' word, "No man cometh unto the Father, but by me."

9

In the mystery of the Trinity, of the hypostatic Union, lies the chief infraction against the faith of Israel, which rests on the certainty of a free and direct communion between Creator and Creation.

10

All theology is to the religious life of prayer, of mystical experience and of good works as the theory of harmony is to music.

11

Since the Deity is *Integritas* and *Incorruptibilitas*

144

personified, humanity has the advantage of one experience over Him: suffering and death. This experience, as the fruit of sin, is of a miserable and pitiable nature. And yet, suffering and death are the deepest experience of created beings; and it is precisely this deepest experience that the Creator does not possess. Herein is revealed to our helpless minds one of the most mysterious reasons for the incarnation of God. The Creator cannot suffer His created being to have any advantage over Him even if it be pain and decay. Something like a longing for debasement and twilight awakens in the Absolute Light. The Lord descends so that man may not be superior to Him even in that which is negative. He descends not only to save the world, but in His very own interest, to taste of death and, within the supernatural order, to renew and sanctify even death, which in the natural sense, is but the stench of putrefaction. By virtue of the Lord Himself, the charnel figure of Death is clothed in purple, and on his naked skull is poised the golden crown.

12

All waiting is waiting for death. Often, when waiting is an end in itself, sheer, stark waiting (for a letter or a telephone call), the element of waiting for death is wholly revealed; then one's own heart-beat hammers the nails into the coffin of time.

13

Living means communicating oneself, that is, turning an inner process outwards. Even God's life means communication. He, too, turns an inner process outwards. He dramatizes His static immutability. The mere contemplation of Himself seems insufficient to Him in the infinitely agitated time about Him.

14

Every motion directed outward from within arises out of insatiability. Metaphysically viewed, this insatiability is the origin of time.

15

There is a divine goad even in the phenomenon of impatience, which in the moral sense is a vice. The impatience in us desires that time should become timeless, that is, that it should return home out of the life-process of creation into the life-process of the Creator.

16

The Deity is, as Holy Writ tells us, Truth and Life. If, however, the Deity is Truth and Life, then outside of Him there can be only lesser truths and lesser life. Not even the Deity can make the parables of His Being of equal rank and equal value to His Being Itself. His self-communication in the universe, consequently, can and may consist exclusively only of analogies. However, analogies, parables, metaphors and similes, are at the same time approximations of, and deviations from, the Truth; for only the Logos itself is identical with the Logos. Consequently, moral weakening, deviation from the path of righteousness, in short, the Fall of Man, are innate in God's self-communication through the parables of the universe, the created things. Failure to achieve perfection, i.e., original sin, thus results logically from the quality of createdness.

17

The Logos descends into the world of metaphors in order to lead them back to itself, that is, to identity, that is, to the ultimate reality.

18

Our personal life is represented to the understanding as a great analogy of transcendency. We possess a subjective feeling of our body. But our body is something entirely different from the subjective feeling that we have of it. It is a thing not only for us, but for itself. Consequently, the body transcends us. Even less than our body does our mind belong to us. The knowledge, for example, that the sum of the angles of a triangle equals 180 degrees, that light travels at a velocity of 186,000 miles per second, that a seventh chord must consist of four separate tones, is not at all my personal knowledge but I am only permitted to partake of it. We are all sitting, in a manner of speaking, at the mind's table which was set long ago, and we dip into the common bowl with more or less appetite. Thus the mind transcends us. But the ego, the person in relation to whom body and mind are transcendent, the personality, is again by no means our own property. We create it as little as we master it. In moments of enlightenment it even appears to us as a plastic, strange and often hostile being over which no power has been given to us. Thus man's ego transcends itself. It is the mysterious image of the Deity within our personal microcosm. It is, so to speak, the most immediate and cheapest God that we can perceive.

19

We revere people by thinking that through our reverence we are praising their deeds and accomplishments, their beauty, their power, their spirituality, their success and their fame. In reality, however, our reverence has a deeper origin than our surrender to the radiant qualities and attainments of dominant personalities. In human triumph we revere a symbol, an analogy of divine splendor. In the light of talent, purity, beauty, or strength that flames forth from a created thing, we unconsciously revere a counterpart of the Supreme Glory itself. Evidences of the groping consciousness of this fact are innumerable in history, from the deification of the Pharoahs and Caesars to the term "divus" and "diva" for the possessor of a high-paid voice.

20

Now and then, even out of the depths of corruptibility, we are struck by a reflection of glory so strong that our heart begins to falter. But how must this glory in the person, origin and goal of all conceivable and inconceivable rapture, grow aware of this rapture and of itself when it is cleft for the purpose of this experience? If there is such a thing as time in the immeasurable duration of God, it may be that it springs forth incessantly in a threefold unity out of the process of the rational realization of truth, of the esthetic realization of perfection, and the erotic realization of love.

21

The final decision as to the faith or skepticism of a man lies locked within two questions: "Can I consider

myself the image of God, or must I consider God the
image of me?"

22

There is no sound argument against the atheist's
contention that man creates his gods, and not vice versa.
That God has created us, we must believe. That we
have created God, we know!

23

The image descends into its reflection for the purpose
of confirming the fact that, in truth, the reflection is
derived from the image.

24

THE LITTLE KITTEN

A little kitten is scampering madly around the room. Cruelly and pitilessly it torments its favorite toy, a rubber mouse. Then it suddenly lets go of its indestructible prey, races insanely across the room, jumps upon the sofa and the easy chair, tries its sharp claws on the cushion, and with its tiny, pointed teeth chews away at a fine coverlet. Finally, with a tremendous leap it plops into my lap, angry because I am not paying it any attention but am reading a book. Now the pages of the book become the object of the tiny, pointed teeth, and I feel the sharp claws on my hand. Soon I find myself looking raptly and with ever increasing curiosity into the creature's beautiful eyes, and I see there a blue void, the wanton, pagan, abysmal unconsciousness of the universe . . .

Half an hour later the little kitten takes an unfortunate jump from the back of the sofa to the floor and seriously injures its front shoulder-joint. In a few days it will die of the injury. But at the time I scarcely notice the little kitten's weak meow of pain. Not until a day later do the people in the house notice that our little pugnacious tomcat is limping along on three legs with his front right paw twisted up. The animal moves about as little as possible. This creature, once so restless, now shrinks quietly into a corner of the sofa, and again I become curiously absorbed in its wondrously beautiful eyes. The blue void, the wanton and abysmal unconsciousness of the universe have disappeared from its gaze. The former emptiness has now become a singular fullness, the fullness of an intelligent communication with me in which the lack of articulate speech can scarcely be felt. Indeed, the motionless pupils of the poor creature's eyes are filled to overflowing with a communicativeness that goes deeper than speech. If I were to say that the look in the kitten's eyes had over-night become human, that wouldn't quite correspond to the truth. The look in its eyes had in an incomprehensible way transcended the deep guilt which every human look expresses. There was no design and no opportunism even in pain. No longer was a reflection of the indifferent universe looking at me but the heart-stirring reflection of the crucified Logos.

Two mysteries move toward each other from opposite directions: the non-suffering Deity must be united with pain in order to become like unto a creature; the suffering creature must be united with pain in order to become like unto God.

25

What can man do for himself in order that he may somewhat resemble the angels? He can act as though time did not exist; that is, not worry in spite of increasing tribulation, not be impatient in spite of roaring monotony, not fear death in the evening in spite of the fatal disease that was disclosed by the doctor's diagnosis in the morning.

26

The German language often links the word "frivolity or levity" (*Leichtsinn*) with the adjective "divine" (*göttlich*), as in "divine levity" (*göttlicher Leichtsinn*). But is not levity a vice? How can a vice be called divine? It can be done because levity is a generally accessible form of experience of *timelessness*. Levity is a very feeble, profane variant of the ecstasy in which saints, mystics and inspired artists lose their sense of time in pure rapture. (It is a phenomenon in the realm of time similar to that which the levitation of the saints is in the realm of space, soaring above the earth's surface, overcoming the force of gravity.) Christ was most human when he was sorrowful: Gethsemane . . . "let this cup pass from me . . ." vexation at the sleeping disciples . . . the outcry on the cross, "My God, my God, why hast thou forsaken me?" . . . In all these moments the Son of Man is entirely caught within the trammels of time. He goes through time without laying claim to the fullness of grace that abides in Him.

Christ is most God when his mood is one of levity; for example, in the words about the lilies of the field and the fowls of the air that sow not nor reap, that toil not nor spin, and yet eat and drink and are more splendidly arrayed than even Solomon in all his glory. In this daring parable which disregards the Fall of Man and its consequences, the Son of Man is farthest removed from economics, which is only another expression for "apprehension," i.e. for the "material."

27

Inspiration, psychologically interpreted, is a sudden simultaneity of the ordinarily sequential. Accelerated associations crowd together; the horizontal becomes vertical; the activity of the soul takes contrapuntal pleasure in itself. The almost divine self-consciousness of one inspired is based on this overcoming of the homophonic, of the "bourgeois" progress of time.

28

Even a gifted poet or artist can reveal something by concealing it. And shall we say that God cannot?

29

What argument is there against the notion that man is the center of creation? Are there any more complex and more differentiated organisms than he? The stars, for example?

I turned to a modern astronomer for an answer to this question. He informed me that the stars are suns similar to our own sun, many of them thousands of times larger and many of them thousands of times smaller. These tremendous, white-hot, gaseous spheres, he told me, are the only form in which matter occurs in that indescribable void that we call the universe. Though astro-physics determines the weight of the stars and their temperatures, the nature of sidereal matter has nothing to do with what we on earth call matter, least of all with the highly organized matter out of which the bodies of living, terrestrial creatures are constructed. Atoms, I was informed, cannot sustain themselves under the enormous pressure prevailing in sidereal spheres and increasing at a high ratio towards their center; consequently, they disintegrate into their hypothethical components, into protons and electrons that travel as waves and rays out into universal space.

"The stars which compose the comparatively sparse population of the universe," concluded the astronomer, "are, accordingly, nothing but inconceivably rarefied condensations of certain chemical elements (hydrogen, oxygen, nitrogen, carbon, and, to name a few of the less common ones, argon and crypton), spherical in form, a raging whirl of exploded atoms engaged in a mysteriously eruptive vital activity."

"Vital activity?" I repeated questioningly. "Does that mean you believe that the stars might be living bodies, mentally alive bodies, personalities, so to speak, which is, after all, the same thing? The latter-day gnostics held the view that stars are the heavenly hosts in material form and that their glowing, eruptive, vital activity represents nothing but the great hymn of praise, the 'Holy, Holy, Holy' with which the angels eternally celebrate the Creator."

At these words, the modern scientist gave me a startled look; then his lips tightened, whether with annoyance or irony I do not know. "Intelligence," he corrected me, "is a phenomenon which is developed only by the most highly differentiated matter in animal and human form, and for the one and only purpose of self-defense and self-assertion for survival . . . The stars, on the other hand, consist of inorganic matter in its most primal and simple form."

"Then organic matter," I interrupted, "highly differentiated, organic matter only exists on the planets? What about the planets, professor?"

"They are extremely rare and exceptional cases in the universe," answered the scientist, "if the prevalent hypothesis is correct. According to this hypothesis, planets and families of planets originate when two stars or suns approach too close to each other in their orbits so that the gravitation of the larger star attracts the smaller one so overpoweringly that part of its matter is torn out of its body, assumes shape and begins to rotate about the larger star in the congealing form of one or more planets."

"Could there be masculine and feminine stars?" I interrupted the astronomer. Again I received a look of disapproval as he continued, "As far as inorganic matter is concerned, it can be charged with either positive or negative electricity, nothing more. Sexual differences and characteristics which serve for the propagation of a species exist only in the more differentiated organic matter, beginning with certain plants."

"Thank you, professor. Forget my stupid question . . . But there's one more thing. If I understand you correctly, it's against the traffic regulations of the universe for the orbits of stars to approach each other too closely."

"Quite right," he responded. "This approach of the stars' orbits and the tearing off of planetary systems thus brought about, are, as our research assumes, among the most unusual catastrophes in the universe, far more unusual, for example, than the explosion of stars (which is in itself quite a rare event) and the formation of nova that is associated with it and that we can observe in our telescopes now and then. The planets, my dear fellow, are a catastrophic anomaly in the realm of matter. And of all the planets, a planet with the earth's conditions of life seems to be the most anomalous of anomalies."

"How can that be, my dear professor?" said I abruptly. "Can it be that the highly differentiated organic matter of which we spoke cannot sustain its life upon the other planets that revolve about our sun?"

"In all probability, no," he answered rather glumly. "On one of them, for example, the atmosphere is too dense, on another it is too rarefied, on a third there isn't any at all, on a fourth the temperature is much too high, on a fifth it is much too low."

"Just a moment, professor. Two stars disturb the harmony by coming too close to each other. The result is that sun-like matter is torn off, catapulted outward and finally cools down slowly. That is, it becomes rock and water, sand and mud, this exiled matter that owes its existence to an infraction, a clumsy violation of law. Is that correct, professor?"

"Approximately, my friend," he grumbled, "if we subtract your mythologically moralizing commentary."

"And out of this exiled, out of this banished, out of this deeply humiliated matter," I continued to question, "does the germ of life spring forth until, in a comparatively short time, it has developed into the human soul that is capable of ecstatically comprehending God?"

"Here you are leaving the paths of science," declared the astronomer, disgusted.

"If, as you say, the earth is already an anomaly, my dear professor, what then is humanity?"

"An anomaly raised to the twelfth power," he laughed contemptuously . . .

When I left the learned man, I realized that science had not lessened my faith but had unintentionally strengthened it. If the earth really is the most anomalous of all anomalies, then for that reason alone it revolves in the innermost center of the universe, a center that can only be a *product of the mind;* for indeed, within the universe, all space and time dimensions are meaningless. And if humanity is really the great exceptional case, as modern theory seems disposed to profess, how easy should it be for everyone to believe that this humanity is the crown and the goal of creation, and that God Himself had decided from the very beginning not to become *Sirius, Aldebaran* or *Cassiopeia* in order to incorporate Himself into a created thing and to have experience of it, but to become something far more rare, greater and more precious, a man.

30

In England, during the most difficult year of the second World War, quadruplets were born to five married couples. The normal ratio of quadruplets in human families, if statistics are to be believed, is one to six hundred thousand. Three of the quadruplets' fathers are soldiers, and of these three, two are members of the R.A.F.

Everyone knows that losses among flyers are the highest. Now will someone explain these supply-tactics of nature rationalistically, mechanistically, or according to the theory of germ cells and of ova, or in some other scientific way? The R.A.F. is, as the most inveterate and confirmed materialist must admit, no simple biological institution. These young men become flyers for intellectual and spiritual reasons but not because of the composition of their blood or because of their sex glands. What power is it then that presents an abnormally numerous progeny to a group of men who have made the decision to risk their lives day and night for intellectual and spiritual reasons (the desire for adventure, the chivalrous impulse, patriotism), a power that blesses them biologically only in order to make up its losses? This power which compensates for a loss originating in a spiritual act of will, must it not also be a spiritual power?

31

The naturalistic-nihilistic mentality is based upon the naive and popular intellectual form of the 18th, the 19th, and of our century, a form of mentality which has permeated the last seven or eight generations with the conviction that the earth is nothing but a ridiculous speck of dust in the universe, a mean little planet shrunk together out of fire into muck, one of the sorriest midgets even among the satellites of that mediocre star, the sun; and in addition to this, situated in a universe filled with billions and trillions of shiny stars, milky ways, and spiral nebulae. Naturalistic-nihilistic man gazes up into the starry sky and does not realize that his weak eyes, in spite of all, encompass and reflect a large part of this sky with all of its well-nigh infinite light-years; but he sighs to himself, as his theory has taught him, "What a maggot am I, what an infusorium, what a germ!"

The following simple thought never even occurs to him, even though it is still within the frame of natural science; namely, that organic life cannot exist on those gaseous balls of light but only on such a mean planet, shrunk into muck, as the one he inhabits; if indeed any other planet than his fulfils the rare preconditions for organic life. He might cling serenely to his naturalistic ideas if his understanding possessed the power of venturing an enharmonic change, as the theory of music calls the reinterpretation of one and the same tuned intonation from one key into a corresponding key, i.e. from F sharp to G flat. He would only have to think: Life is a product only of the earth or of earthlike satellites. Life not only has the tendency of lasting within itself, i.e. of perpetuating itself, but no less a tendency of becoming more subtle, variegated, and complex. The most highly complex form of life, the gray, convoluted mass of the human brain, is the bearer of the spirit. Accordingly, even as a biologist, one could prove that all development of organic matter is conditioned by the life instinct to attain awareness of itself. Hence, the spirit is the self-awareness of life which the universe produces under certain extremely rare conditions. This spirit, this self-awareness of life, however, is primarily revealed, as Aristotle observed, in the elementary functions of astonishment and questioning, "Where does the world come from? Why does it exist? Where do I come from? Why do I exist? Whither am I bound?" Preformed in the gray mass of the human cerebrum lies an answer that must already have been created into the lowest cellular form of organic matter to emerge finally in the self-awareness of life, in the spirit. It is the answer that comes from the experience of causality: if the last-nearest phenomenon has a reason (*causa*) then the first-farthest phenomenon must also have had a reason (*causa*). At this point, however, by means of a kind of enharmonic change, the naturalist already finds himself on the path that leads beyond nature . . . And modern astronomy, as her foremost luminaries have clearly calculated, corroborates the notion that this universe in which we are is not eternal but was created at some definite time. And they even reveal this time in numbers and figures (200 trillion years) and thus acknowledge a prime cause by means of which uncreated being has produced created being.

32

In the image of God made He man (Genesis 9, 6). This truth would be in direct, blasphemous contradiction to that other truth which says that God is not flesh but spirit, uncreated being, hence invisible, unimaginable and inconceivable, that is, if the Word of God had not become flesh in the image of man. Incarnation is, consequently, not only an act of loving grace but an act of logical necessity; not only an act compassionately involving the world but an act clarifyingly involving the Deity Himself in order to give evidence and reality to the phenomenon of man's Godlike image. Thus God created the image before the model by creating Adam before Christ, who was before Adam.

THEOLOGOUMENA

33

When we bend over an atlas of zoology and carefully examine illustrations from the insect world magnified ten times the natural size—e.g. an ordinary cockroach or a tropical spider—then our heart stands still at the grotesque sight; then the "good Lord," the *"bon Dieu"* of naive, popular piety seems to us the most superficial of all trivialities. What? Is it possible that a white-bearded Supreme Sovereign, an affable Old Man of Heaven who, after all, reduced everyone to reason and everything to orderliness; is it possible that He could have conceived these positively obscene shapes, these long, revolting antennae, these horse-like heads, these jaws out of which grow many-membered mandibles, these dorsal shells and greaves, these nauseating bead-eyes or pop-eyes, this frightful hairiness of the limbs? In view of the inexhaustible realm of forms of insects and worms, the gnostics seem almost plausible to us with their doctrine that nature is not a direct creation of God but was subcontracted to the *"En Soph,"* the *"Ens Primum et Ultimum,"* the "Ancient of Days," to a demiurge, a sub-creator, a department head beyond time and space, good and evil, who with masturbatory exuberance transforms into life his wondrously beautiful and wondrously horrible day-dreams. A glance at nature, if we are capable of feeling profoundly enough, shows us not the nearness of the Creator but his un-attainable, unilluminable, impenetrable remoteness. The same glance into the confusion of created forms, how-ever, also shows the necessity of the incarnate Son of Man, of this mighty Interpreter between us and the impenetrable. Without the Messiah, the sensitive and speculative man of our time would be, nay, *is,* in despair.

ON THE SACREDNESS OF PROPERTY

1

Property is sacred in the same sense as our body is sacred. Even the consciousness of ownership that we have of our body is, to a large degree, an illusion, or more precisely, an aid to life granted to us by the natural order, not different from the consciousness of any other ownership on earth. The physical and chemical elements of which our body is composed belong to the body only as a loan; they are "common property," they are derived, so to speak, from the national wealth of the universe. Individuation, that act which configurates the unique and non-recurrent ego, appropriates these elements as private capital. Accordingly, in individuation itself lies the proof and justification for the fact that all property must represent a personal and temporary appropriation from the reserves of the collective economy, an attachment without which all life would be impossible.

2

I did not make my skin nor did I give some equivalent value in exchange for it. And yet my skin is mine. In the same sense my shirt must be mine although I did not sew it, and my house must be mine although I did not build it.

3

"Whoever does not work shall not eat." This sadistic principle which maliciously confirms a deplorable state of affairs, contains one of man's deepest humiliations. It reduces the metaphysical worth of my life to economic worthlessness. What? Can it be that my right to life and the value of my life consist of nothing else than the production of fodder, with the guarantee of a share of that fodder, physical and spiritual? The above principle casts a merciless light upon the whole paltriness of the socialist heresy that profoundly debases us humans even though it incessantly pays lip service to our human dignity.

4

Socialism, too, has its eschatology, its great finalities, its beatific vision, i.e. its vaunted, classless society. For man is man, and cannot do without the notion of a Kingdom of Heaven, even in the most trivial of eras.

5

The embittered plebeian can neither understand nor endure the thought that the supreme goods of life, beauty, genius, and intelligence, are undeserved and must be undeserved! But we kneel before these goods precisely because they are unearned, remote from the effort of will and the economic cycle. Wherever we meet these goods, the pure atmosphere of God's glory, which is the inexhaustible reservoir of the dispensation of grace, breathes upon us, quickening the breath of our faith.

6

If we consider individuation, the development of the ego, for what it is, namely the supreme creative process within nature, the ego necessarily appears to us in its highest differentiation and refinement, as a crystallization of life, as the goal of all of God's creative activity. We are not only images of the form but also of the essence;

that is, no matter how every earthly ego may differ in kind and degree in its ego-ness, it still remains an analogue of the substance of all personality. Since, however, the substance of God is personality, then logically the personality must also be the substance of the image. But what could personality be other than property *par excellence?* No high degree of philosophic thought is required to recognize clearly that a person is all the more intensified a personality the more imperiously and absolutely he can say of certain forces, traits of character, qualities, gifts and goods, "THEY ARE MINE." Hence the idea of ownership is anchored in the very archtype of all ego-property, in God!

7

Stirner's well-known exaggeration, "Property is theft," is, of course, not quite unfounded. In the world of metaphors, parables, and similes, which this earth is, all property (including our ego, which is the integral of all property) denotes, if not theft, at least an appropriation and selfish accumulation of general elements and goods. Even if we disregard the chemical and physical substances which constitute our body, the spiritual and mental components of our ego have likewise been acquired and appropriated, partly from the heritage of our more immediate forbears and partly from the total, arduous achievement of all humanity. Rightly viewed, the unique phenomenon of our ego is founded solely on infinite permutation, that is, on the changing manner of acquisition of all these elements and goods. In the world of metaphors and similes there is, therefore, no real personality—for only God possesses that—but there are

merely reflected and mirrored personalities. The pangs
of conscience which humanity constantly experiences in
regard to the concept of property emanate from the
presentiment of this frailty. Communism has its origin
not only in the envy of groups and masses who feel
themselves cheated of their claim on life, but no less in
a religious reaction to these pangs of conscience, to
which Jesus Christ once gave the words, "Sell whatsoever
thou hast and give to the poor, and follow me."

8

"Sell whatsoever thou hast, yes, even your ego." That
is the sacred, paradoxical demand of religion, which tries
to lead man from the illusory personality of the meta-
phorical world to the true reality of God. "Sell your
personality," cries communism, "and surrender its capital
to an impersonal power, to society." It must be admitted
that the conscience referred to above has sadly degenerated on its way from "Sell whatsoever thou hast" to
"disappropriate the others."

9

We are neither more nor less proprietors of our ego
than, say, a member of a lending library is the proprietor
of a book that he has borrowed. All moral requirements
which refer to our own ego are rooted symbolically in
the obligation of that member to return the borrowed
book at the end of the loan period in decent condition,
without blemishes, without torn or missing pages, and
with as few dog-ears as possible.

10

Suicide includes two mortal sins. The first, the breaking of the commandment, "Thou shalt not kill," can sooner be forgiven on grounds of self-defense against the unbearableness of life than the second, the unfaithful administration of someone else's property which has been temporarily entrusted to us and which has an eternal history and everlasting mission beyond consciousness.

11

RESURRECTION OF THE FLESH

The rose's fragrance, which outlasts the rose, longs to be once more united with its mother that gave it forth. The body of the child of man is one of our "mothers." That is why the mothers of us children of men are so concerned about our bodies.

12

When I wander further and further and deeper and deeper into the landscape of my inner life, I come at last to a final indivisibility. I shall call it *the fundamental emotion,* for it is not a matter of knowledge but of feeling. This fundamental emotion—it is the vessel of grace—decides whether I may believe or whether I cannot believe, just as it alone decides whether poetry moves me or not.

13

Whoever in the night suddenly thinks the terrible thought that his own body is alive only by virtue of incomprehensible grace, that the lurking powers of destruction within him are momentarily held in equilibrium, —to him, with bated breath, the entire universe seems a house of cards.

14

The form of the cross is embedded in the human form, says the mystic, as a frame of iron in concrete. It is, so to speak, the inner staff with which the human form makes its pilgrimage. The form of the cross, says the naturalist ironically, was derived by the Romans from the human form, for criminological purposes.

To be derived, it must first have existed, says the mystic.

But the naturalist laughs: if the lizards or insects had been victorious in the struggle for existence and had snatched the mastery of the earth for themselves, then the lizard-Romans or insect-Romans, in order to execute their criminals, would have had to invent some other, more serviceable gallows than the cross.

The fact is, responds the mystic, that *man* was victorious, and not the insects; and with man, the cross embedded within him.

This is one of those conversations in which both speakers are always right because their words run parallel.

15

The trinitarian relationship among Father, Son, and Holy Ghost has its organic and functional equivalent here on earth in the triune synergism of brain, heart, and nervous system. Upon the Father depends contemplation, upon the Son emotion, upon the Holy Ghost activity, the transmission of neural energy to the muscles.

16

What applies to property and its most explicit representative, the body, roughly applies to matter. Matter is sacred. It is sacred because it represents the sole vehicle whereby the Creator can prove His existence. Of course, without this vehicle, God would be no less than He is, for the infinite cannot be decreased by subtraction. But no matter how meaningless the finite-created may be in reference to the infinite-uncreated, there would undoubtedly be something missing from the former without the latter: the responsive mirror of a creature consciousness outside of, and opposite to, the Divine Consciousness. To our presumably sacrilegious human imagination occurs the more than obvious thought that that Uncreated Being may have need of a Created Being in order to emerge from its subjectivity and realize itself objectively in the creature. Thus the full growth of consciousness of the Deity, the *visio beatifica,* would be created into the created being as an ultimately attainable goal. That is why, as the bearer of this inborne ultimate purpose, matter is sacred.

17

Even the reading of modern astro-physics could convince one of the sacredness of matter. James Jeans interprets the history of creation naturalistically, as he calls it, by speaking of "radiant energy" which "streamed into space" about two trillion solar years ago, a period of time which is, cosmically, not at all incalculable. This radiant energy, the most immaterial veil of matter as expressed by the high negative exponent of its formula number, this radiant energy, compared to which the astral substance of spirits from Elysium seems hippopotamic and elephantine, this radiant energy stirs our imagination far more sacrally than naturalistically. Its "streaming in" or "streaming down," as Jeans puts it, could easily amount to a confirmation of the biblical history of creation. To be sure, the "space" into which the astronomer permits radiant energy to flow is an unauthorized *hysteron proteron*. For it is not until a first *something* flows into a second *something* which previously was *nothing* that this second *something* becomes what it is. It is the creation of radiant energy that first makes space out of the space into which it flows; and since this radiant energy consists not only of one point but of many widely separated points, it divides the space from the time which is between these points, provided that motion is operative from one to the other. And God spoke, "Let there be light." This light, however, was substance, that is, radiant energy. And it was through this substance that space and time first came into being.

18

We spoke of a transcendent purpose that the Uncreated Being must have given to the Created Being to accompany it on its way: the full awakening to consciousness of God as a personality in the mirror of creature personalities originating and developing out of the matter that has streamed into space (the human soul created for immortality as a universal goal). Can there not also be inborne into created matter a more immanent goal in addition to this transcendent goal? Whether there is a migration of souls may be open to doubt; there certainly is a migration of bodies of matter. A large part of what originally "flowed down" and "streamed in" has gathered in its two-hundred-trillion-year biography well-nigh innumerable experiences of form and essence. The primordial incorporeal radiation of matter sank down to the solid bodies which inhabit the earth and also, perhaps, some other satellites of the shining stars. The radiance, whose top limit is of a wave length of 1.3×10^{-13} cm., is transformed into something that does not radiate but can only be measured and weighed by the crudest standards; that is, it is transformed into our own human bodies. And yet it is precisely in its lowest stage of "degeneration" that this primary radiant energy first begins to become spiriual, i.e. to ask "why" and to feel guilt. If some day at the end of time this degenerate matter should again rise up into radiant energy, streaming out of space as once it streamed into space, it could no longer be the same that it had been in the very beginning. At least part of it—and presumably the most essential part— will have been transmuted by suffering, wonderment, and conscience.

19

An old poem taught in the schools and entitled "The Monk of Heisterbach" contains, if I remember correctly, the beautiful line, "To God a thousand years are but a day." This is a tremendous understatement. If this time-bound and space-bound universe, i.e. the matter that fills its space, will at the end of several trillion centuries, have been consumed, vaporized, and will have flowed back from the *nothing* through which it was made space (as modern astronomers prognosticate), then the world will not only not have lasted for a day, that is, the time which the satellite Earth requires to rotate about its axis—but not even for an instant. For, to God, 800 trillion years and the quadrillionth of a second are

170

equally short or equally long, i.e. neither short nor long, but without any extent. Perhaps God created three hundred quintillion different universes *before* he created this universe, or, seen with the eyes of His timelessness, *at the same time* as He created this universe wherein we dwell upon our earth; and perhaps He still creates them and takes them back again and creates them anew. But it is not these things, beyond all measure and imagination, that are important to us. What is important is only the conviction that that matter (radiant energy), which in the course of universal time crystallized into the intellectual, spiritual, carnate, human personality, comes from God and returns home to God. This is, as modern astronomy must admit, a simple, clear, sensible, logical possibility. Out of this conviction flows the most singular of all comforts: nothing can happen to us, for although forsaken upon the doorstep of time, like foundlings, we are God's own children in eternity.

20

The stupidest of all inventions of nihilistic thinking is the so-called "impersonal God." Confronted with this non-personal God, one is tempted to bless the personal non-God of the honest atheist; for the concept of a spiritless and senseless world created by nothing and by no one, and existing nevertheless, is for all its ghastliness, more acceptable than the idiotic notion of a kind of extra-mundane and autonomous power station that creates and feeds all things without ever at all having been invented or operated by a creative Mind. The impersonal God is the most wretched reflection of technologized and thought-weary brains, the modern old folks' home of senile pantheism.

BETWEEN HEAVEN AND EARTH

21

Christianity concedes a certain right to egocentricity. If my ego represents such a precious possession that it may some day be the contemplating partner of the Infinite and Eternal, outside of time, then this ego well merits that one should be concerned about it and not let it go contemptuously to the dogs. But as everything here below is paradoxical with reference to the divine final goal, this ego cannot be saved by hoarding it stingily but only by spending it extravagantly.

22

The deterioration of property is profoundly related to the mass production of goods. We can thus easily use economics for a study of metaphysics. In olden times property was the symbol of the physical ego. Inseparable from the idea of property was the notion of durability and permanence. The wedding gown still served an old woman in death as a burial dress. The craftsman guarded his tools as he would the apple of his eye, for it was difficult to replace them. Everything produced was distinguished by costliness, massiveness, and the fact that it was destined to be inherited. Economic life was rigid and static, thus correspondingly reflecting the era's state of consciousness, namely that of Scholasticism. For the exact opposite of an "ideological superstructure" actually prevails. Historical frames of mind have a material substructure: the Above is reflected in the Below, heaven is mirrored in the pool and not the pool in heaven. When theology disintegrated, when man began to grow arrogant (for countless reasons it had to be so) and stepped out of his material poverty and spiritual wealth into material wealth and spiritual poverty, then the value of exchange, of money, began to grow independent of products. Capital not only is not property, it is almost the absolute opposite of property; it is nothing but *potential mass-produced goods,* the purpose of which is less to satisfy wants than to create them, in a vicious circle, so that potential mass-produced goods, that is, capital, might again be accumulated. The innermost meaning of mass-produced goods is quick expendability so that the goods, increased by margins of profit, can return to their potential state, that is, become capital again. Thus, in highly logical conformity, the apparent antagonist but actual twin brother of capitalism, collective socialism, teaches that all property is a presumption to be rejected. This also includes the human ego which is the quintessence of property, although neither is identical with the other. But socialism is not even aware of the higher logic that its view expresses. This is the formula of the vicious cycle: loss of God, i.e. loss of ego, i.e. loss of property, i.e. capitalism, i.e. mass-produced goods, i.e. quick expendability, i.e. shoddiness, i.e. unsatisfying satisfaction of wants, i.e. tragic unrest of the human spirit, i.e. the alternative choice between anarchistic and totalitarian forms of existence, i.e. perpetual war.

23

Capitalism is nothing but the *natural* expression of the Fall of Man in the economic realm of our age. Since it is a natural expression it has the advantage of genuineness in contrast with all the other frantically artificial and speciously moral systems (autarchy, state socialism, planned economy). It is freely confessed disorder, arising from a primordial error which in its (capitalism's) opinion is not retroactively reparable. To believe this error reparable, Capitalism is much too naive and much too intelligent—like life itself, the opportunistic enjoyment of which is capitalism's only end—a better end than the isolationist, hate-charged pseudo-morality of collectivist principles that torture and kill in the name of a more equitable division of property.

24

Perhaps the most atrocious desecration of the ego since the beginning of history is the modern form of feudal serfdom: Man is no longer his own proprietor, but the property of a state from which there is no appeal, a state which is employer and depriver of employment, provider or bailiff of starvation, father confessor, educator, corruptor, stool-pigeon, judge, prosecutor, defender, juror, and hangman—all in one person. As long as even a single state on earth exercises this unnatural, diabolical, soul-destroying, character-breaking power, just so long—despite the best-laid peace plans—world war will reign in perpetuity. No amount of opportunistic hypocrisy can ever alter this situation.

25

One of the most frequently advanced proofs against the continuation of the human personality despite death is the contention that the animal too has a soul. There was a famous Russian biologist, Professor Pavlov, who with impressive zeal made it his business to demonstrate that man is but an animal and not one whit better. Pavlov wasn't satisfied with the general experience that teaches us again and again that the animal exists in man no less than man exists in the animal. This experience, of course, leaves a back door open to metaphysics in its *purely human* aspect, and hence was not at all satisfactory to the good Professor Pavlov whose *quod erat demonstrandum* consisted exclusively of the main and fundamental principle that man is an animal, that he is essentially identical with an animal and that his soul is an animal's soul.

So as to be able to demonstrate his proof with particular brilliance, Pavlov perpetrated a petty fraud, one of those small aids and corrections of "chance" that the assumptionless critical and exact sciences are so fond of when it is a question of faultlessly deducing an *apriori,* desired result from the object under investigation. The Russian biologist chose as his object of deduction the only animal that is no longer wholly an animal but one that through millenia of association with humans has become an imitator of man. Pavlov chose a dog. After sixty years of indefatigable experimentation, the noted scientist succeeded in clearly demonstrating that the household companion, imitator, and opportunistic observer of man can be just as melancholy, phlegmatic, sanguine and choleric as the master whom he imitates. But unfortunately, the great biologist must have been a very poor philosopher, for he didn't even notice that he had deduced from the image in the distorted mirror nothing else nor better than the existence of a reflection in the distorted mirror. However, we must gird ourselves with patience and wait until Pavlov's pupils demonstrate the existence of claustrophobia in rattlesnakes and homosexuality in bullfrogs. But even this experiment would not tell us the least about man and his soul.

26

Property (*proprietas*) both as a term and as a concept

refers to man's *subjective Self* ("Ego"). We have tried to define as well and as incontrovertibly as possible the extent to which property is sacred and at the same time illusory. Possession (*possessio*) both as a term and as a concept refers to man's *objective Self* ("Thou") and, indeed, in its most concentrated form, for woman with reference to man and for man with reference to woman. Possession is even more imaginary and illusory than property, but at the same time it is probably less sacred. For the Ego is a property that leaves man only when God pronounces the judgment of eternal death over him. The Thou leaves man, man leaves woman and woman leaves man at every instant, and indeed this Thou can act in no other way, for after all it actually is an Ego and exists objectively as "Thou" only in the view of another Ego. A concentrated Thou originates through the fact that a demanding Ego takes possession of another, dispensing Ego. It is an act of occupying and of being occupied, a martial act as the wisdom of language suggests, although it is this act that makes life really worth living. Even the fact of lust betrays the deeply equivocal state of affairs whereby it is not two flames that interpermeate each other as they are consumed but two integers, entirely delimited and circumscribed, which by clashing with each other generate that subjective warmth leading centripetally inwards, and producing the orgasm of love, that illusion of mutual interpermeation after which, as the Romans maintained, so quickly follows the disillusioned *tristitia* of all living beings.

When we said, comparatively speaking, that the subjective Self (Ego) of property is more sacred than the objective Self (Thou) of possession, we did not express the true relationship quite correctly. The Ego is not more sacred than the Thou but merely sacred in a different way. In the Ego is incorporated God's most immediate and fervent concern about us. In the Thou is incorporated the world's great moral concern about us. Without the Thou, the Ego would have no love and, as a maimed cripple, would thus not even be an Ego.

27

Death is an expropriation of the less essential constituent elements of the ego. The chemical compounds which the body has acquired are re-interred with the body in its biological form; and it is the same with the acquisitions of consciousness and memory, and everything from the external world that is mirrored and reflected inwards, the vocabulary of the universe, so to speak. What, then, remains? Is it the mirror that included within itself all that was mirrored and reflected, is that the ego that remains? No! Every mirror becomes an absolute void when the reflected image disappears from it. What, then, remains? The innermost part of one's inner self, i.e. the unique and non-recurrent capacity of being awakened by God to vital response. This is what led to the coining of that profound phrase: *individuum ineffabile*, the inexpressible personality. But what is it that, for us, is ineffable and inexpressible? Everything that has no content of experience, i.e. no inward reflection of the external world. Hence, death deprives me of all that is mine insofar as I am still capable of saying "you," (as "you, my hand," "you, my physical energy," "you, my talent," "you, my erotic pleasure"); and there is left to me a one and only essence, to which I can say "I," although I cannot express it.

A FEW WORDS ON SIN

1

Sin is the mysterious epitome of perversity, of the perverse life. It reaches from the supernatural order, to which it belongs as a mystery, into the very midst of our natural existence from which it can be read as clearly as from the face of a clock. The most substantial sin is that which we commit against ourself, especially against our own body. The offense against our own body includes the sin against the Creator. Hence, with the sin against our own body as a model, we can study and learn to know the nature of the entire complex of sins.

2

Our body is a part of the universal order created and preserved by God. Rightly viewed, it is itself a self-contained universe entrusted to us as a limited but sacred property. Its health and its welfare depend chiefly upon ourselves, disregarding the external destinies and perils that threaten it. There is an instinct innate in us not to desecrate or, to put it more profanely, not to damage the order of the major and minor circulation of the blood, of metabolism, and of the endocrine secretions created by God and incorporated into us. But God has given us even more than this physiological instinct of distinguishing between good and evil as regards the borrowed property of our flesh. He has set up a guard of warners and watchers. It is, *sit venia verbo,* the *body-guard of pain,* from the slightest discomfort to the full-panoplied torment, whose intent is to inform us that the God-willed order of nature in our body has been disturbed.

Pain is the sentinel who calls out the Halt-who's-there to Death. The Church teaches that death is the fruit of sin. But it can equally be said that sin is also the fruit of death,—which means that the final goal, the greedy and ultimate intent of sin, is death, non-existence, the most negative manifestation of polar remoteness from God, if the word manifestation were not absurd in this connection. This suicidal tendency of sin is made manifest, in so far as we analyze it in its grossest form, in its relation to our body, to the external part of our ego.

3

God has appointed the bodyguard of pain to warn us whenever the God-willed order in our body is endangered by outer or inner causes. The demonic antagonist of God, however, is again master over a bodyguard in us which serves its ultimate purpose, absolute death. This bodyguard of the evil antagonist consists of morbid temptations, irresistible seductions and wicked impulses that are ready at any moment to gain dominion over our nerves. What a drama . . .

4

The Church teaches that we offend God by our sins. In the word "offend" is hidden the anthropomorphic circumlocution of a state of affairs that reaches far and completely into our reality. Between God and us prevails an inevitable, metaphysical automatism. By our sins we primarily hurt ourself. But in hurting ourself, we hurt (offend) God in His image. We afflict the love in Him, which is the spring of our existence, whenever we muddy the waters of this spring.

5

Every sin, even the most brutal, is a spiritual sin. That is why animals cannot sin.

6

The artist is the purest antithesis of the saint. The saint sacrifices his ego to God; the artist sacrifices himself to his ego.

7

The most terrible curse of illness is based on the fact that a man's entire attention is concentrated on his stricken ego. Even a slight toothache raises a barrier about us that we can hardly penetrate. During an attack of colic even the most charitable person is incapable of any altruistic act. Illness as a fruit of original sin intensifies to the extreme our sinful tendency towards egotism; and the impotence of our will in the face of an ego-pervasive pain seems to be sufficient justification for our innate egotism. In reality, however, the curse of illness reveals a dual intention. It invites us either to hell or to heaven. It is like an ultimate X-ray examination of the supreme value of a man. Illness either delivers a man, bereft of soul, to matter or, offered as a sacrifice, it liberates his saintliness by letting his ego grow more transparent, more soaring, more encompassing, until the hour of death. Not only does hagiography teach us this, but the sight of many a secular sick man. How great is man's destiny if he can transform even the most horrible of all curses into a blessing!

8

I have never forgotten the strangely sweet smile of

mortally wounded men from the days when I was in the war. The deadly shot suddenly revealed upon the face of a soulless brute a childlike gracious spirituality which must have slumbered under the hundred layers of brutality and vulgarity. The God-man emerged from between the parting clouds of dying.

9

There are diseases of condensation (cancer) and diseases of attenuation (tuberculosis).

10

God asks us to love him not because he needs our love of Him but because *we* need our love of Him.

11

Serious cases of mental diseases are a natural proof of the existence of hell. For in two ways only are the boundaries of reason crossed: by faith, that mirrors Heaven, and by insanity.

12

The states of insanity of a hell that no Dante has ever described are a total lack of logic, and a totally false logic. Both spring from their polar remoteness from the Logos. The total lack of logic expresses itself in a thoughtful man's chokingly cramped feeling of impotency at never again being able to restore order in the confusion of things. The totally false logic is an incessant, stubborn, and pedantic strutting about in the labyrinth of the most sophistical false conclusions.

13

Life, in its remoteness from God, is a kind of habitual

penance in the depths of which lies a natural hope for absolution from sin.

14

How peculiar it is that even in the enlightened world there are still people who believe they are the victims of injustice.

15

How and where in the world could man ever be right? All during his lifetime he is in a desperate state of trying to justify himself, and in his truly enlightened moments he actually knows it.

16

One must have sunk up to his neck in human filth and impotency in order to realize most profoundly that this life could never be endured without the idea of supernatural punishment and supernatural aid.

17

Sometimes a supermundane justice glows forth out of worldly, logical consistency, like the pale gleam of gold in California's desert sands.

18

Of all creatures it is only given unto man to create disorder. The further a creature is removed from man, the more unswervingly does it remain concentric with order. Disorder is nothing but the converse of another mysterious phenomenon: *freedom.* The twin-like, automatic affinity of freedom and disorder offers a natural proof of supernatural truth which is both hidden and revealed in the biblical story of creation. Man, to whom God awards freedom, cannot resist the overpowering craving for anarchy. By the gift of freedom, God has *overestimated* man, because this gift includes within itself the temptation to disorder and disobedience, that is, to the Fall of Man. But, alas, it is the very overestimation of man by God that really makes man man.

19

" . . . And lead us not into temptation." Is this sixth petition in the Lord's Prayer not an unexampled blasphemy? What? Shall it be said that Infinite Goodness *leads* us into temptation, plays the same game as the prostitute on a street corner, as the receiver palming off stolen goods in his hideaway, as the political demagogue in the meeting hall, yes, even as the devil in person? . . . And yet, the dread sentence, " . . . And lead us not into temptation" is in the most exalted prayer in the world, the prayer that the Son, who is the Father, addresses to the Father, who is the Son. Not "Let us not be led into temptation" but "Lead us not into temptation." The Son knows His Father. Only the Son may intimately interpret temporal weakness to Eternal Strength, may whisper the burden of sickness and fear to Him who rejoices without suffering, the state of waiting for something that always proves to be nothing but death, to that State of Ineffable Peace. The Son prays and teaches us to pray with a faint shadow of loving melancholy, " . . . And lead us not into temptation." Perhaps it means, when translated from the language of prayer into the interpretative language between time and timelessness: "Lord, do not overestimate us as long as we are in the flesh."

20

The form of deterioration is the measure of the eminence from which a creature may fall. A stone merely erodes, a plant withers, an animal or a human body must decompose after death; and the more complex the organization of such a body, the more horrible the process of decomposition. Immortal creatures, of course, the incorporeal or transfigured-corporeal angels, cannot erode, wither, nor decompose; their decay can be achieved only spiritually: they become *evil* by denying the epitome of life. Satan is the spiritual state of decomposition of the fallen angel, Lucifer. Folk legend knows of that. The devil's smell of sulphur and brimstone indicates that all evil is a kind of process of putrefaction, i.e. a teeming and extremely vital negation of life. How strange! The more spiritual, the worse the odor!

21

Out of the inexplicable gap between organic and inorganic matter freedom and sin spring forth.

22

The inorganic! What is inorganic? Does it not consist of the same protons and electrons as the organic? May it therefore not be only a human subsumption? Its metaphysical formula should read: The inorganic is the obedient which has been deprived of the possibility of disobedience.

23

In the spectrum of truest and gravest sickness, the

stricken one feels, in enlightened moments, a strange ray of suspicion that he is perhaps pretending just the least bit or that he is outwardly showing his undoubtedly miserable condition with some overstatement. This suspicion is based on the supernatural recollection by our imaged being of the healthy (what an absurd word), of the deathless and painless form of being of our original image. In our strange suspicion of pretending lies the premonitory half-consciousness of the fact that sickness, and with it, all worldly pain, is not a reality of the first degree. This half-consciousness is at the same time the matrix of all higher irony and victory over the temporal.

24

There is a great advantage in all sickness. Although sickness, in the organic and metaphysical sense, denotes the victory of disorder over order, it creates simultaneous with this victory a new order, of course, not quite the right one, but nonetheless and undoubtedly, an order. The heedless and anarchic daily course of the sinner is suddenly subjected to a strict routine; the sinner is presented with a new childhood and a new innocence, and not only through the penance which sickness exacts from him. His weakness deprives him of his freedom, and with it too, of the opportunity of being the scoundrel that he is. Nature has temporarily arrested him in the name of God. Who knows whether he is already sitting in the death-cell, from which there is only a short way leading to the gallows, or whether he is simply detained for questioning and will soon be released again? In either case, no matter which, he is given another chance to mend his ways.

25

At the foot of a steep, high, rocky mountain, a man is lying upon a comfortable reclining chair such as is used in all sanataria. He is a sinner. He knows with all his being that he has not only received the stern task of immediately climbing that rocky mountain but that it is desperately necessary for him to do so. His diseased lungs and his weak heart would not prevent him from venturing on this imperiously demanded undertaking even if he should fall or in some other way be destroyed while climbing. But in addition to all this he has only one leg and therefore is quite a hopeless case. He remains there lying motionless in his comfortable enervation, feels conscious of guilt and at the same time is angry with God. However, his consciousness of guilt, his anger, and even his oneleggedness make him secretly proud, whereby his sin, failure to do the impossible, becomes more singularly intensified.

26

All life is a phenomenon of compensation, and hence a breath-taking peril. To feel this to the utmost is already "decompensation."

27

Whenever the cold banality of materialism darkly spreads over the human spirit, as may happen over and over again from one era to another, then the mystic truths close up like lotus blossoms after sunset. Then it is not we who no longer know these truths but it is they that regally do not permit themselves to be known.

28

But perhaps the matter is different. Perhaps the mystic truths do not close up out of regal contempt for the all-pervasive, cold banality of materialism. Perhaps, in the dispensation of divine providence, they deliberately yield to this materialism so that man should not always gaze into the heavens but probe the infinity of earthly details with zest and zeal. Science, a looking-away from God, may be a moral demand that God makes on man so that he might dream less. The sin against the Holy Ghost consists of the fact that man, bent over the microscope, not only looks away from God but, possessed by the arrogant demon of the knowledge of details, willfully drives Him out of mind and memory.

29

Within the next few years there will be many changes; for in the interim, the snobs of nihilistic intellectualism will finally have noticed not only that they have so long been serving the most inane form of triviality but that they have been completely outdated. A snob can stand anything except being out of date. I foresee a panic, a mass rout through all emergency exits into a new mysticism. What a fine mess that will be! At the beginning of the Eleusinian Mysteries the chiefs of the mystics called out *"Tas Tyras!"*—"To the doors!" Which meant that the watchmen were given the task of barring the entrance of the as yet uninitiated neophytes into the sanctum. Tomorrow, unfortunately, there will be no one obeying the call, *"Tas Tyras!"* to bar those snobs from the gate.

30

The four stages of the mystic rites of Eleusis were called, first, *Katharsis,* Purification; second, *Photismos,* Enlightenment; third, *Teleisis,* Fulfillment; and fourth and highest, *Theosis,* Deification. The mystic of Eleusis was obliged to subject himself to the most strenuous ascetic exercises in order to attain (or not to attain) that one of the four stages to which he felt himself destined. Eleusinian asceticism, like every other asceticism, was based on the profound experience that the body, i.e. matter, with its wilful, tyrannical impulses, must be overcome as far as possible by purification, renunciation, torment, mortification, and complete release, so that man might be made worthy of a more spiritual state than the one to which he was born. All this is related here in order to expose the old liberalistic nonsense which continually asserts that it was only Christianity through its obscurantist and even perverse hatred of the senses that invented the hostility to the flesh and put an end to the Dionysian, physical and erotic joy of Greek Classicism. It is upon this obtuse insult against Hellenism that much of Nietzscheanism is based. No! Millenia before the Greeks, a natural revelation had already made ancient man aware of the system of balances between body and spirit.

31

Elsewhere we spoke of the "fundamental emotion" as man's ultimate and indivisible way of feeling, out of which his entire conduct emerges. However, since all creation is dualistic, we must not only recognize this fundamental emotion as the vessel of grace, as we have done, but also as the glowing coals of damnation out of which smoulder the hate and fanaticism of hell; for in this fundamental emotion is also rooted politics.

32

The original cause of the experience of sin lies in our feeling of conviction that nothing in this world is really profane and that everything is sacred because it flows forth out of God. The holiest of holies is our relation to the Creator, which is manifested in a most real sense in our relation to His creatures. Why else would an incessant feeling of guilt mark our relations to our neighbor-mortals (insofar as we are morally awake at all): the relation to our wife, husband, father, son, daughter, brother, sister, friend, servant, not to forget the relation to our own ego,—why else should we feel guilty if we did not, in all these creatures, hurt the love of God that is in us? If the feeling of the holiness of life is buried, as has been required by the vast secularization of the last three centuries, then the higher power of love is emasculated within us, then our consciousness of guilt is stultified into a utilitarian hangover that quickly melts and evaporates like wet snow.

So too, true poetry can only develop out of the naive feeling of conviction that suffuses us from head to toe, that everything in the Here is sacred because it stems from the Hereafter.

33

The basic formula of all sin is: frustrated or neglected love.

34

The virgin crushes the serpent's head with her foot. What a symbol! Even the purest and most refined must come *into direct contact* with the filthiest and most depraved in order to destroy it.

35

Just as illness provides an opportunity for self-clarification, so too does old age. Of course, it is by no means true that we are free from sexuality in old age; but as years go by, barriers arise between our impulses and their gratification, barriers that make sinning difficult. An old man often suffers torment, but he knows what he is, what he looks like, how he functions, and what he has to offer. And so he is ashamed, to his own greater honor. Perhaps at the last moment this enforced ascetism will be credited towards the old sinner's salvation, even if there isn't anything else to speak in his favor.

36

The damned is no less an inmate of hell because he does not believe in it.

ON SEEING GOD

1

The intoxicating joy of seeing, the heartfelt delight in nature, is the earthly, sense-bound, preliminary form of that heavenly activity of the soul which theology calls *"visio beatifica."*

2

But not only the joy of seeing, no, every pleasure of observation, every impulse of investigation, every interest in creatures, every gratification of contemplative sympathy preforms the soul's activity of *"visio beatifica."*

3

To the soul that is permitted to see Him, God will not be an intellectual image but a dramatic performance. A dramatic performance with music! Perhaps the delight of opera is something that, as a weak, preliminary form, points towards this splendid mystery.

4

At a dramatic performance the onlooker is entirely ego and entirely non-ego. That is the great mystery of identification.

5

Seeing God is the highest possible act of identification; that is, a supernatural mode of being entirely I and entirely You; and out of this identification stream eternities of delight.

WHAT TATIAN, AN APOLOGIST OF THE SECOND CENTURY A.D., SAYS:

In the beginning was God. But the beginning is, as John the Evangelist records, *the power of the Logos.* The Lord of all things, who Himself is the foundation (Hypostasis) of the universe, was alone when as yet there was no creation. Insofar, however, as all power of visible and invisible things was in Him, He encompassed within Himself the existence of all things by virtue of His Logos. Through the free decision of His onefold and uniform being, the Logos appeared out of Him, and not without a cause: the Logos becomes the first creation of the Father; and we know that it is the beginning and origin of the universe. But what it became, it became by virtue of its *distinction* from the Fatherly Being, not in consequence of its *separation* from the Father. For what is cut off is forever separate. But what exists by virtue of distinction partakes of the Father's self-determination, and has not made Him poorer out of whom it was taken. For just as many fires can be lit from one torch without diminishing the flames of that torch by the lighting of the other flames, so too did the Logos not deprive its Begetter when it issued forth out of the power of the Father. In the same way I, too, am speaking and you hear me, and yet I am not deprived of my Logos when the sound of my voice conveys it to you; but, as I send out my Logos it is strengthened because it creates an orderly sequence out of the inchoate subject matter in you.

ON CHRIST AND ISRAEL

1

If Christ is Truth and Life, then the Jews are the everlasting witness in the flesh, of this Truth. Without this living witness, that wanders, persecuted and scourged through the whole world, Christ would sink down into a mere myth, like Apollo or Dionysos.

2

The Jews are, moreover, the witness in the flesh of the parable about "the cornerstone that the builders have cast aside."

3

"The first shall be the last" also points towards Israel. What Moses first said of them, "It is a stiffnecked people," includes the strange fact that Israel cannot metaphysically understand nor portray itself. These two spiritual activities, understanding oneself and portraying oneself, presuppose a characteristic whose exact opposite signifies stiffneckedness and arrogance, that is, remaining steadfast within oneself. It may be a mystery of the divine intent of history that Israel must interpret itself falsely both from without and within, otherwise the first would not have to wait until the end of history in order to be the last.

4

The Messiah signifies conquered Jewish subjectivity. The Messiah is He who comes to interpret Israel aright to itself and to the world. It is impossible for Israel to acknowledge the Messiah, nor even the Prophets "until the time has been fulfilled," that is, actually not until the end of time.

5

Even for a Jew who considers Jesus Christ to be the true, historically-realized Messiah, and even the Son of God, baptism and conversion are inadequate. He holds an entirely different attitude towards the coming of Christ than that held by the "nations," that is, the Christianized heathens. He belongs to an entirely different order than they. The Jew is not "curable" through baptism and faith alone.

6

Every Jew of every variety and of every era, as a member of supra-temporal Judaism, has refused to recognize Jesus Christ, has thrust aside the hand of salvation held out by God, with the result that the final salvation of the world has been postponed; and the Jew, as a second Adam, has in modern times lost the Paradise that already was almost within reach. And just as Adam must carry his world-history with him as penance, the Jew cannot be absolved from his Jewish world-history because of his non-recognition and rejection of the Messiah. He must therefore live as the great exceptional case, who belongs neither to the "nations" nor to Christ, who builds his Church with the stones of these "nations," that is, the *Corpus Christi Mysticum*. Baptism and acceptance into the Church, no matter how secure theologically, is a concealment of the natural and supernatural facts of the matter. The Jew, as a sufferer, has the right to conceal his situation; but no matter how much he may in individual cases believe in

194

Christ, he is as tragically barred by the profundity of the facts from being a Christian as he is from being a German or a Russian.

7

From time to time this tremendous paradox is acknowledged by the great minds of both religions: that the predestined recipient of salvation is the only one who is excluded from salvation until the last day but one of world-history.

8

Israel, however, according to sound theology, is also at the same time the origin of all world-history from that moment on when God and man crossed each other's paths in the sphere of reality. As Adam was the father of the first genus of men, and Noah of the second, so Israel is the father of the third mankind.

9

Israel is chosen, not only in the sense of a Chosen People; an omniscient and omnipotent Providence has offered Israel still another role which Israel has not refused and which may one day, at the end of history, bring it renown and honor. Israel had to assume the role of antagonist so that the drama of salvation of a spurned Deity could unfold in time and reality as the sacrifice of the *Agnus Dei Qui Tollit Peccata Mundi.* With the assumption of this wicked role, Israel, as a people and as a separate entity, sacrificed itself for the Divine Being, so that the Divine Being might sacrifice Himself as a Universal Being for the nations. In this way, God's Providence actually condemned Israel to reject God Himself for the salvation of the whole world.

10

And so the people of God, as long as there will be a Christian history, that is to say, until the end of time, will be like the hapless actor in a provincial theater, who must play the villain and who is booed off the stage by the naive audience. And how indeed should a naive onlooker be able to distinguish between the invisible hand of authorship and the visible drama?

11

If religious and secularized Judaism considers the incident of Christ only as a painful episode of its own history which had best not be discussed at all, it is quite foolish although not quite incomprehensible. It is more incomprehensible that theologians should persist in over-simplifying the problem of Israel and in ranking it among those peoples susceptible to missionary conversion, like the Papuans and the African Pygmies.

12

Antisemitism is, as its contemporary form demonstrates in the great modern heresies of nationalism and socialism, no human weakness only, as for example, the racial hatred between the white and colored peoples, but a metaphysical phenomenon. It is a form of resistance to Christ, directed against the point of least resistance. Israel's mission from the very beginning has been to force to the attention of the nations the great paradox of the inversion of naive, heathen values, the great demand: live *counter* to your sinful nature.

Jesus Christ is also, in addition to everything else that He is, the fulfillment of this mission of Israel.

13

Israel, disregarding its own consciousness, is to the Messiah, in fact, as mother-of-pearl is to pearl. This is by no means merely an historical fact but primarily a metaphysical and mystical fact. Even the *"Mysterium Magnum"* which was in God's plan of salvation from the beginning has clung to the peculiarity of His creation; when this mystery entered world and time, it subjected itself to the historical conditions of world and time.

14

Jesus was not born of Greeks and Indians, but of Jews. What is decisive about this fact is that it is not so much a question of consanguinity as of conformity and conspirituality. Our Father in heaven, of whom the "nations" speak, is the God of Abraham, Isaac and Jacob, who revealed Himself on Sinai, who spoke to the Prophets Elijah, Isaiah, and Jeremiah, who became Man and died upon Golgotha. This God reveals Himself in an uninterrupted climax to His People with whom He carries on an unending dialogue to this very day. In Israel's soul alone the knowledge of this God was preformed, from Abraham to Jesus. Israel's soul was and is the concave mirror which reflects the rays of this Deity out of a mysterious conformity into the *camera obscura* of this world. The empirical fallibility, weakness, obstinacy, even the temporary depravity of Judaism change nothing in this intelligible fact. Israel not only was but continues to be the mother-of-pearl, just as Christ remains the pearl. The hatred directed against Israel is, accordingly, no hatred of the evil traits of a certain species of human, but, driven by envy, merely uses these as an excuse to hate Israel as the created cause of the unbearable paradox between Sinai and Golgotha. Thus, within a Christian who is an antisemite, it is the mechanically-baptized but essentially unconverted and uncircumcized nature that hates its Messiah, its Redeemer.

15

The idea of the Kingdom of God on earth is generally characterized as typically Jewish, and is rejected. I must take exception to this view which I do not find to be quite correct. It goes without saying that Israel like every human community (to which we should add that it has existed for an unusually long time) has gone through all the guises of history and historical ideas. But neither in the Pentateuch nor in the Prophets, neither in the Talmud nor in the Cabbala is there anything to be found similar to the idea of earthly perfection as the goal and end of all things. Where this idea is encountered in the above-mentioned compendia, it appears as an eschatological premise of salvation (as the fulfillment of the individual soul and the community soul). To be sure, man is, in the conception of the Old Testament, completely independent of Divine Grace; yet he can obstruct it or hasten it by his cooperation or rejection. Isaiah's most famous words, those of the sword and the spear which will one day be beaten into the scythe and plowshare, have an eschatological significance, not a profane and political one. They mean that when man one day becomes united with the Divine Will, then the space-time tragedy will be dissolved and the *"Olom,"* the aeon of salvation will have arrived. The Here will fuse into the Hereafter. Thus does Isaiah envision the Kingdom of Heaven, as at another time he envisions the King Messiah as an unknown beggar and suffering bondsman. And Ezekiel, no less, was the first to give us a classical representation of the resurrection of the flesh.

The idea of the Kingdom of God *on earth* as an aim of Jewish religion is, consequently, a hostile interpretation of our time. It is nothing but pure secularization. Certainly there were times of national distress in which the Jews conceived the Messiah as an avenging King of the Sword (second and third centuries A.D.). But that passed quickly, again and again. In the seventeenth and eighteenth centuries the Messiah was thought of eschatologically and apocalyptically, even when a false Messiah appeared like Zabbatai Zevi. Not until the late nineteenth century was messianism secularized down into social pathos, and by none other than the Jews themselves, who had become skeptics as a result of the *Ersatz*-religion of science. This *Ersatz*-religion of science, however, completely changed, not only Israel alone, but the whole world.

16

A Jew who steps up to the baptismal font is a deserter in a threefold climax. In the first place, he deserts, in a profane sense, from the side of the weak and the persecuted, from a human unit intended for a particularly ignominious and painful kind of history. This step seems, to say the least, not very noble and generous, even if it may involve no lower opportunism than the salvation of his own soul.

This same Jew, in the second place, deserts not only the defamed and tortured community of present-day Israel; he deserts from Israel's deepest origins, from Abraham, Isaac, and Jacob. - It is a difficult and questionable step to turn one's back even on a profane people. But it is inconceivably difficult, especially for a religious person, to turn his back on the People of God that have suffered so much along the way, from Abraham's persecution in Egypt up to the Era of Nazi-pogroms, eternally slaughtered for the sake of their God.

But in the third place, this Jew who goes to the baptismal font, deserts Christ Himself, since he arbitrarily interrupts his historical suffering - the penance for rejecting the Messiah - and in a hasty manner not foreseen in the drama of salvation, steps to the side of the Redeemer, where he probably does not at all belong, according to the Redeemer's holy will; at any rate, *not yet,* and not here and now.

17

What would Israel be without the Church? And what would the Church be without Israel?

18

Israel is more than a nation; it is an historical and biological order, - a mendicant order even, in spite of a few rich individuals, - an order into which, according to the decree of God, one enters by birth, never to be released until the last day but one.

19

Election: "And ye shall be unto me a kingdom of priests, and an holy nation." (Exodus 19,6). That is, ye shall set yourselves apart! That is, ye shall set yourselves apart from all others! That is ye shall set yourselves apart not *merely* as one nation is set apart from another! That is, ye shall set yourselves apart from all others *precisely in that* which joins them in common!

20

It is one of the inscrutable mysteries of human history that the Jews are always the dupes of their attempts at establishing themselves. In the days of antiquity, long before the advent of Christ, they attempted to establish themselves as Egyptians, Babylonians, and Greeks, a fact treated on almost every page of the Old Testament. But always their guises were ripped off them in shreds so that the pale, suffering flesh of Israel gleamed forth again and again. Their attempts at establishing themselves in modern times were called, "Enlightenment," "Cosmopolitanism," "Liberalism," "Socialism," and "Nationalism." They ended with the great European and Polish blood-bath.

Only two other genuine possibilities of establishment remain, towards which the Jewish columns are crowding with the incorrigible obstinacy of ants seeking to escape; for after all, a man must live: American democracy and Russian proletarianism. The foreboding soul shudders at the thought that the great interdiction for Israel to be anything else but Israel cannot stop before these two forces.

21

The Jews' wild, political, scientific, and artistic passion for innovation has its root in the metaphysical impatience of Ahasuerus, in his burning desire that historical time should come to an end. The Jews are historically over-impetuous, they are effervescent, they rush along precipitously; and therefore they are also bad politicians, because they are too hasty.

22

In casting the roles for the drama of salvation, God did not hesitate to assign to Jewish Jerusalem the part of the rancorous, bickering plaintiff; but to Aryan Rome he assigned the part of the bureaucratic judge and brutal hangsman. And so each was inescapably saddled with his proper share of the guilt; and which of the two would dare to usurp the right of giving himself airs over the other?

23

That Israel was preserved for the purpose of bearing witness was recognized by the great Pascal. "If the Jews had all been converted," he wrote in the 749th of his *Pensées,* "we should have only questionable witnesses. But if they had all been exterminated, we should have no witnesses at all." But not even Pascal realized the core of the problem, for, by the decree of God, it seems destined to be concealed even from the profoundest of pagan Christians. Israel, bearing negative witness to Christ on earth through its suffering of persecution and dispersal, will be the positive state's witness in that last trial beyond history, when the infinite Father-and-

Son love of God will be ultimately revealed, for the promise made to Abraham is still valid.

24

From what has been said, some might think that I am claiming for Israel the prerogative of nobility and of a privileged position among mankind. That would be a grave mistake. I would never translate the corresponding Hebrew term of the bible as "chosen," but only as "set apart." Of course, the relation of God to His People, and with it a large part of Jewish history, is enacted in the realm of mystery. The other part, however, which is enacted in the realm of profane reality, by no means gives the Jews any cause for pride, arrogance, or, least of all, presumptuousness. They are as recreant, as stiffnecked, and as impenitent as ever they were in the time of Moses. No other people have plunged with equal readiness and so completely head-over-heels into the naturalistic-nihilistic betrayal of God as have the Jews. And worse than that, no other people within the last hundred years have so sentimentally and opportunistically secularized the divine sense of life as they.

We know that supernatural grace is not granted on account of natural merit. We even know that in many cases the obvious lack of an individual's merit almost seems to be the prerequisite of election for grace. To this very day the sacred and profane history of Israel are related to each other as grace is to lack of merit.

25

In various newspaper items concerning a Jewish political party, one meets with increasing frequency the expression, "The Hebrew Nation." He who has ears to hear, let him hear. The overtones of these words sing out to us: "Away with God! Away with our sacred history! Away with our guilt! Away with our mission! Away with the exalted status reserved for us to the end of days! Let us be like the Bulgarians, Roumanians, or Albanians, a small nation among other small nations. Once, four thousand years ago we were nomadic desert tribes who called themselves Hebrews. In those days Jacob had not yet wrestled with the Angel and had not yet received the name "Israel" for that struggle in which his thigh was wrenched out of joint. We want to become again exactly what our tribe was before Jacob wrestled with the Angel.

26

One of Israel's strangest transgressions is the fact that because of its type of character and form of being, it invites the sin of antisemitism on the part of Christians and heathens. This is a paradoxical instance of unconscious and involuntary invitation to evil, for the purpose of one's own harm.

27

We know from hagiography that the bestowal of grace is generally balanced by some excessive burden of suffering. Is there any greater history of suffering than Israel's? And is the passion of suffering not the soil of those trees that are intended to grow up into Heaven?

28

As I now re-read these lines on Christ and Israel, written some years ago, I feel like closing my eyes and forgetting everything. To what a subtle dilemma of escapelessness has God condemned those creatures whose eternal favor He had promised to Abraham? What way of escape do they have? The way of liberalism? Who would not be ashamed of its superficial and false cheapness? The way of nationalism? Self-deceit and self-destruction! One becomes a Hebrew nationalist in order not to have to be a Jew any longer! The way of orthodoxy? There is no retreat from life into fossilization, even if it be a holiest fossilization. The way to Christ? It is blocked by profane barriers and by the barriers of a deeper knowledge. (But herein I have touched upon a mystery which I do not feel strong enough nor wise enough to interpret validly.) There is no way out! And yet the God of Abraham, Isaac, and Jacob is in our time performing a sign and a miracle on the person of Israel that overshadows the biblical miracles of retribution. Within a single generation God has made Israel's enemy greater than Pharoah, Nebuchadnezzar, and Antiochus, all rolled into one. And before this generation tasted death, God has plunged the archenemy into the abyss of humiliation and scorn and filth, as no enemy before him, so that the promise to Abraham and his seed might be fulfilled again and again, at least in a negative sense. What a triumph, one might think. What infinite jubilation in the hearts of those in whom the divine phophesy has been again and again so wondrously revealed in our very day! But how could triumph and jubilation be felt by a vacant-eyed, tattered old graybeard who, spade in hand, is staggering about in the Ukrainian steppes, to find his dead and to bury them?

29

Only to the oldest soul, refined by living and suffering, does God speak: "Thou shalt belong to no one nor to any thing, to no party, no majority and no minority, and to no community though it serve me at my altar. Thou shalt not belong to thy parents, nor to thy wife and children, and likewise not to thy brothers and sisters; nor shalt thou belong to them that speak thy language, and even less to them that speak another language, and least of all to thyself. Thou shalt be only *mine* within thy world. But how else couldst thou be mine than by living unassumingly in thy world, like any other people, and yet not belonging to that world?"

30

Complete human detachment is the first psychological symptom of spirituality. It is a two-edged symptom: in its denial of love, a premise of hell; in its absorption with the first cause (*prima causa*), a premise of heaven.

31

A signpost, battered and warped, stands at an autumnal crossroads. Its right, outstretched, wooden hand half-points uncertainly upward toward the cloud-racked sky; its left, drooping, wooden hand half-points downward toward a fallow field. It is whipped by gales and gusts of rain. But it is oblivious to them. It is a stubborn wanderer that enroute long ago froze into a signpost. Those who hurry past in the early dawn glance at it and read the name and direction of the destination that the raised right hand indicates. They will reach the destination that it points out with inde-

fatigable zeal, while it stands at the road, growing more
warped and more battered, until it will topple over one
day. Or will it bestir itself at last and follow those to
whom it has pointed the direction toward the destination?

32

The foundation for the "theory of correspondences"
was already laid by Paul the Apostle in his epistles.
According to this theory, later developed more fully by
the Church Fathers, the most important characters and
stories of the Old Testament foreshadow the revealed
or hidden truths of the New Testament. They are
sketches and blue-prints of these truths and at the same
time a code by means of which the story of salvation
can be better read and understood, that holy story which
the christian world history considers itself to be till the
Day of Judgment. A magnificent and splendid example
of this "theory of correspondences" is the story of
Joseph and His Brethren, although I no longer recollect
whether it was first treated by Saint Irenaeus, Saint
Clement, Origen or Tertullian. Joseph is a sketch of
the Messiah, a model of Christ. He is much closer to
his father's heart than are his brothers. He possesses
greater talents than they. He can rightly interpret
dreams. The interpretation of dreams stands for the
Messiah's power to perform miracles. The brothers
(the twelve tribes, i.e. all Israel) are offended at Joseph's
interpretation of dreams, an interpretation whose seemingly overweening presumption drives the brothers into
a rage, not unlike the way Jesus of Nazareth's self-
assurance (The Son of God) later incensed the rabbinical
theocrats in Jerusalem. The brothers cast Joseph into

the pit from which he arises, as Jesus Christ arises from his sepulchre. But the brothers did not kill Joseph, any more than the Jewish people under Tiberius killed the Roman offender with the mocking superscription *"Jesus Nazarenus Rex Judaeorum,"* who was executed on the pretext of having violated Roman sovereignty. Joseph's brothers, or to be more precise, his brother Judah (Judas), sells him for some pieces of silver just as one of the twelve disciples, who bore the same name, sold Jesus for some pieces of silver. As a result of this sale, or betrayal, Joseph came among the heathen (as did Jesus), i.e. both became estranged from their own people. By the fact that his interpretation of Pharoah's dreams turns out to be true, Joseph is revealed for what he is and rises to the highest rank next to the sovereign. And in an exactly corresponding way Jesus Christ rises to the highest rank next to the Lord in the heathen world which accepts his miracles as true and real. Joseph's reign becomes a blessing for Egypt. During the seven years of plenty the great steward provides for the seven years of famine by filling his renowned granaries with inexhaustible quantities of wheat. Corresponding to this but on a higher plane, Jesus does the same by filling the granaries of eternity, the churches, with the inexhaustible wheat of the Eucharist . . .

So far so good. For this is about where we now are in the story of correspondences, and we cannot even know exactly whether we are in the seven years of the fat kine or in the seven years of the lean kine, although there seems to be a good deal of evidence in favor of the latter. However, the Joseph story, or better, its reflection in Christian world history goes further, and it is probably no accident at all that a great novelist of our day has brilliantly re-invoked it. But, of course, no one, at least not to my knowledge, has carried the parallel to its conclusion in accordance with the theory of correspondences; for what will still happen between Christ and Israel belongs not to the past but to the future history of the world. At any rate, the corresponding motifs between the first half of the Joseph story and of the Christ story are so clear and unforced that, as a kind of mechanical prophesy, one might also venture to apply them to the second and not yet fulfilled half.

The Bible tells how the entire world was afflicted with hunger and famine from which Egypt alone, despite her blighted crops, was spared through Joseph's foresight. Now, what does this hunger and famine signify if we follow the comparison between Joseph and Christ? The state of emergency is, of course, meant to be spiritual. The whole world is starving for want of food for the soul and spirit. Man's hunger for a higher meaning in the world cannot be appeased by existing naturalistic ideologies which are but the withered ideologies of the blighted crop. Only in Egypt—which in a parallel sense means: only in the world which is under the stewardship of Christ—is there still any grain to be had. But even there the grain no longer *grows* but is only *stored up*. Even in its very own realm Christianity exists more as a preserved than as a powerful, living force. It is more a matter of tradition and rote than of experience and faith. Nevertheless, in an epoch of absolute blight the world is necessarily dependent upon the granaries of Joseph and Jesus Christ, the churches. From all over the world starving people journey to Egypt to buy bread. In the same way many people journey from the non-Christian or no-longer-Christian world to the church to apply for food of the soul and spirit. And so too, Joseph's brethren, Jacob's children and the children of Israel, at their father's bidding, journey to Egypt to acquire bread so that "they may not die of hunger." The father has not forgotten his lost, favorite son. But the brothers, the sons of Israel, have well nigh forgotten Joseph or, expressed in modern terms, they have suppressed him into the subconscious. Joseph, on the other hand, and, correspondingly, Jesus Christ, in their exile have not for a moment forgotten their brothers, Jacob's children. Both suffer on behalf of each other. But the more conscious always suffers more than the less conscious. Joseph, although raised to the highest position as governor of Egypt, suffers deeply when he thinks of his father's children, his brothers, of their guilt and of the long separation. And so Jesus Christ suffers when he thinks of Israel. Only the great wound in Joseph's soul explains the deceitful and yet sublime drama that he enacts to punish his brothers, a long and perilous drama, before he makes himself known and with trembling voice speaks those words that still echo through the ages down to our day: "I am Joseph, your brother." - Corresponding to this and in a constant spiritual climax, there will be between Christ and Israel when the time is ripe enough, i.e. lean enough, still many a dramatic vexation and many a sublime drama before the ennobled brother makes himself known to his humbled brethren, and his voice begins to speak to them and *out* of them: "I am Jesus, your brother, the Messiah . . ."

Since the first or past half of the parallel matches, by analogy the second or future part would also have to be fulfilled and, indeed, approximately as we have outlined it in broad, fleeting strokes. The most interesting detail of the analogy, however, would not be revealed until after the drama of recognition and reunion of those who are so profoundly separated. Joseph allots to his brothers, as is written, a province of their own in which to dwell, and to graze their cattle, the land of Goshen which, to be sure, is under the scepter of Egypt but is more separate and independent than the royal domain proper. In the intensified spiritual parallel of the theory of correspondences, this can signify nothing else than that Israel as a whole will enter the church of its Messiah but will not lose its identity. For the sake of kinship and of bearing witness it will be preserved as a separate entity even when it disappears into unity.

33

Take comfort, Israel! Martyr, thou, not only in the sense of torture and persecution but even more in the sense of duration. Israel, who art ashamed of the martyrdom of duration and hence, in order to veil thy heart, playest the part of a snob of actuality and contemporaneity and hast become a fanatic adherent of all easily-perishable values! Israel, who would like to erase the thousand-year traits of sorrow from thy countenance by the arrogance of a purely worldly morality, take comfort nonetheless. God can sooner revoke His revelation, yea, his world, than His promise to you. What a ridiculous God He would be, who made a promise that He, in His omniscience, must have been ready to break as He was making it? Believe not thy foes when they say thou art forsaken like a useless slave, an old outworn servant who is summarily driven out of the house. Do not believe it, Israel! Between thy God and thee there is an unsettled reckoning that will one day be settled in thy favor, when grace will have struck the balance.

PROFANE ADDENDA

1

What we call superstition is often but the wavering flow of heated air around the jutting flame of faith.

2

Only the extreme skeptic knows nothing of superstition, and for the most part, even he is not untouched by it. Just as the soul is never quite identical with the consciousness, neither is his faith or skepticism.

3

The meaning of the ritual covering of the head by the priest lies in some heliotropism of the spiritual world. It is protection against the sun, a tropical helmet against the Divine.

4

Of all dreamers, the primitive realist is the one who dreams most deeply; for he is so irretrievably wrapped up in the dream of his supposed reality that the thought never even occurs to him that he is dreaming.

5

My life! Again and again I come as a stranger into a strange city. Even in the Hereafter I shall be only a visitor or a refugee.

6

I have a strange feeling in my heart. Be conscious of every moment—so it reminds me—try whenever you can to write down all you feel and see. You are not wholly *of* this world nor wholly *in* it, but like a guest of long-forgotten times. Upon these self-assured days, shade in the nuances of your observations and sensations, like contraband of the I-know-not-where and I-know-not-when.

7

Organic matter, late-born out of the congealing and cooling of the planet, is perhaps a holy attempt of matter to return home again, by the detour of earth's dark life, to a radiant life of higher power than that of the sun.

8

That great, historical exorcism called Christianity seems to be receding further every day; and the demons, with shrill confusion of voices, are breaking their chains.

9

LUCIFER'S COMPLAINT

"The other gods, prithee, will not let me be God."
"That, my dear fellow, is the artist's lot."

10

God assumed the form of man in order to reduce it to an *ad absurdum,* the while raising it to glory.

11

Man is, in the profane sense, an exaggeration.

12

The liberal era has confused equality before putrefaction with equality before God.

13

The only advantage of the hunted is that he can never be the hunter.

14

To be a stranger is a prodigious occupation requiring diligence and skill.

15

No man can be wise against his own wishful thinking. He can only act as though he were.

16

The basis of every supernatural faith is an act of will.

17

Unto the blind the world is blind;
Unto the deaf it speaks no word;
So one will think all faith absurd
Who in himself no faith can find.

18

The greater the vacuum, the greater the speed.

19

All is only metaphor. But why do metaphors suffer?

20

Can it be that the great knowledge of all geniuses in the arts and sciences is only the whispering of those who died in ancient days, and who are now trying to help their living brothers by means of the clairvoyance of a few among them?

21

Fate is the photographic negative of human personality retouched by cosmic influence and divine control.

22

Religion is the everlasting dialogue between humanity and God. Art is its soliloquy.

23

God does not condone what men condone. Men do not condone what God condones.

24

It is indeed remarkable that every transiently rented room, every hotel room into which we move, immediately assumes the character of our personality, for good or for ill.

25

How do I ever manage, in the twinkling of an eye, and with my few writing utensils, to conjure upon any desk the confusion of my soul and its helplessness before God?

26

To know nothing of shipwreck and ocean but to swim from spar to spar with half-closed eyes as though in a swimming pool, that's what I call the technique of living.

27

From one little goal to another little goal with heaving breast, that alone helps man to overcome his monstrous plight.

28

All pacifistic ideals become suspect of sentimentality after a short time, because in the face of general, natural death, the struggle against unnatural death must again and again lose its value.

29

If, in every human relation into which we enter in life, we were to recognize honestly the task set before us, and fearlessly measure our daily failure, insanity would be the most merciful consequence.

30

The safest wealth is lack of needs.

31

The personality's aphelion and perihelion to eternal things: even the believer is often at a perihelion to Christ, and sometimes at an aphelion.

32

The nationalistic reversion from a universal God to a tribal God is worse than atheism; for a Nothing is more real than an idol.

33

"A nation, in a nationalistic sense," said that clever publicity-hound, Graf Sternberg, "is the abstract collection of all the vain and antipathetic characteristics of a definite species of man for the purpose of conscious imitation of this model."

34

The Sublime is not to be generalized. That is why

no form of human community is ever an expression of the Sublime. At best it can only be a humble recipient of the Sublime.

35

The Alpha and Omega of human intercourse: Grant a chance of superiority not only to your enemies, but now and then to your friends as well.

36

The more ego, the more death. That is why the death on the cross is so deeply beyond understanding; because there never had been so much ego in a single individual as was in Jesus.

37

What is beyond the world? The entire universe can be only a section of the world.

38

How easy it is to reduce all moral nihilism to absurdity. Nietzsche, for example, asks "What is good?" and answers himself by saying "To be good is to be brave!" But bravery is an empty virtue. What really matters is the purpose of bravery. Otherwise there would be no difference between the hero and the gangster; for the cornered gangster holding a superior number of policemen at bay, is also brave. The criminal who will not betray his accomplices even under the tortures of the third degree is not only brave but presumably braver than the average soldier who at least is never alone on the battlefield. "To be good means to be brave," says Nietzsche, in these words foreshadowing national socialism.

No! To be brave means to be good!

39

Democracy in a certain well-known sense requires that everyone must cover the road leading from the cave-dweller to the subscriber to philharmonic concerts, all in his own lifetime and career, and without the slightest strain on the nervous system.

40

It is better for an intellectual work to be obscured by failure than by success.

41

Success has the character of a cat. It won't come when coaxed.

42

Success wants to be undeserved.

43

It may be that the planets, in comparison with the madly whirling atomic state of the matter composing all the other solar stars, are a kind of exiled matter, like cosmic penal colonies sent to Siberia.

44

Twilight is the decay of light. *Decay* is the twilight of matter.

45

How could we die were we not immortal?

46

The test of an artist is that he must have the power

of projecting himself into the future as a constellation that gathers lesser names around it and relates them to itself.

47

As in every great work of literature, a lofty, theological symbolism can be shown to exist in that story within a story, the "Arabian Nights' Entertainment."

The Sultan, Shahriyar, is outraged to the core of his being by his wife's unfaithfulness and revenges himself upon the entire sex by marrying a different maiden each night and having her put to death the next morning. Parents hide their daughters to escape the tyrant. But Scheherezade, the Vizier's daughter, spared by the Sultan himself for an unknown reason, offers herself to him of her own free will, and saves her life and the lives of her sisters by relating the tales of the Thousand and One Nights, tales that are never completed by morning, so that the royal listener's curiosity is never satisfied.

To the male instinct for destruction and the thirst for revenge of an insatiable will to action, we have here the contrast of the *higher craftiness of art,* the feminine play of imagination that holds, enthrals, and finally dissolves the murderous principle of world history, blind, illusion-obsessed realism. Thus it is only imagination that tames empty activism. Thus it is only the spirit that, night after night, cajoles life away from destructiveness.

What a symbol of the artist! To tell the story, to sing the song for one's very life!

48

Nothing can be more definitely past, nor more historically pathetic, than an old theater poster, outliving a monarchy somewhere on a forgotten wall in the suburbs.

49

God is total time, i.e. eternity. That is why satanism is also concealed in the worship of time-segments. Reactionary satanism praises the past, revolutionary satanism the future.

50

The realm of art lies in the deep dusk created by cosmic darkness and human twilight.

51

Pascal makes a distinction between writers (*Schriftsteller*) and speakers (*Sprechsteller*). In that connection he suggests that the gifted speaker receives his inspiration from his listeners. The gifted speaker, in a sense, evokes a genius from his listeners that neither they nor he possesses. To the author such magic is denied. In his icy solitude there are no listeners from whom anything might be evoked. Opposite him sits none other than his attainable ideal of perfection, a prudish dame who generally shakes her head disapprovingly.

52

In the thirteenth century, a scholar would take into his hands with reverence a manuscript copy of the *Aeneid* that he had borrowed from a monastery library. Out of the first products of the art of printing a sacred thrill was transmitted to the reader, who did not as today loll back comfortably in a bed, but sat before the volume, with beating heart, on a hard wooden bench. Today the price of a well-printed book is not much more than that for a sandwich or a bottle of beer. Intellectual broadening and progress? Certainly! But is this progress not just as much a decline? Reading requires effort and concentration. And why should anyone exert himself and concentrate at such low cost? From the disparity between price and value, it is always value alone that suffers. Already the art of reading has today become much more rare than the art of writing.

53

It may be that a new kind of picture-writing is now coming into existence, a type of writing intended to relieve people of the effort of reading the letters of the alphabet and integrating them in their minds into a thought or a story. The film conveys emotions without the medium of concepts. A new primitivism is at hand, with new, demotic hieroglyphs and an ignorant, childish fear of the abstract.

54

"Whoever reads too slow or too fast," says Pascal, "will not understand anything." He has characterized the reader of the twentieth century.

55

To be a human being means to set a parable over against life.

56

Restraint in literature? Yes! But it must be like drained land that has been reclaimed from the waters of passion.

57

Woe unto the revolutionary who does not know that the fighting fronts of necessary revolt are constantly changing, and with them, the targets for his weapons.

58

Death is frozen time. Time is molten death.

59

In the cleverly pointed phrase language takes the sting out of truth.

60

The victory of the scientific state of mind results from the fact that it eliminates all feeling of guilt.

61

Women are like the soundest savings banks. The bad habits, traits, and opinions of the men with whom they have lived accumulate interest in them at an astonishingly high and sure percentage.

62

There they go, those weazened hobgoblins, with lanterns at their belts, with their Jewish noses not quite in the symmetric center of their faces, and with giant baskets on their hunched backs. And they shout, "Bring on the whole burden of humanity! We will carry it, all right!" And yet they scarcely have the strength to drag themselves, dying, into a damp corner, squinting piteously from between their thick lids to see whether some kind hand might, perhaps, fleetingly caress them.

63

When a man gets older he is tempted to divide people into those that detest him because they need him, and those that despise him because they don't need him.

64

Law is man's protection against man by means of man for the sake of God.

65

Only the modern refugee knows what it means to fall out of the mousetrap of imprisonment into the mousetrap of freedom.

66

The materialistic philosophy of history: What? Is it possible that the train is actually running? Yes! Only the timetable was completely off.

67

"How are you?" This form of greeting shows that humanity is as sick as a dog. For only a sick person would be asked such a clinical question at every meeting.

68

I wear an armor of my scars. They grow constantly thicker and harder. If I live long enough I shall become invulnerable.

69

Only an anachronism has any chance of outlasting its era.

70

When one observes commercial nudism and nude commercialism in all of their innocent im-pudence and shamelessness, one really discovers what old and subtle cultural values are hidden in prudery and hypocrisy!

71

Naked Truth (*nuda veritas*) is the harlot-bride of the barbarian. Civilization begins precisely with the need to conceal something, i.e. with the consciousness of original sin. (Adam's fig-leaf is the first document of civilization.) But reversion to barbarism begins precisely with the uncovering of that which had been concealed, that is to say, with psychology.

72

Shame and chastity are the sure thermometer on which one can read the erotic power of a person, a society, and an era. The higher the mercury of shame rises, the more ardent and true the erotic impulse is. The modern cult of the body is the invention of frigid, graceless, unerotic and insensitive peoples whose basic excitement of "buying and selling" exceeds all other excitements.

73

Satan's deepest impulse is snobbery (and this applies to all satanists, i.e. average modern intellectuals). There is one thing that satan has really achieved. He is more *elegant* than God. The shrewd theology of scholasticism was already well aware of the fact, for it designated the state of existence of satan and his infernal crew by the wonderful and almost Byronic expression of *"negative transfiguration!"*

225

74

In the vagaries of historical dialectic it sometimes happens that satan's elegance, his negative transfiguration, loses its brilliance. Then a paradoxical state of affairs emerges, and God becomes the goal of satanistic snobbery, and the satanist seems to be affirming God. A curious form of blasphemy!

75

The naturalistic era, whose political credo lay *everywhere* in socialistic nationalism, advised the individual, "Man, be yourself!"

The next, the dawning era, for which no name has yet been found, but which is striving for the unification of great complexes, is preparing to teach, "Man, be yourself *and* be your opposite." This is an exalted doctrine that may perhaps enthrone Christianity anew.

76

Eloquence, rhetorical skill, and brilliant mastery of language do not at all arouse our admiration but rather our embarrassment, as though we were witness to venal unchastity.

77

The true "good society" is always either in the past or in the future.

78

Does the dress coat exalt the waiter? Or does the waiter degrade the dress coat?

ON BEING STARED AT BY A MOUSE

That mouse cost me a sleepless night. Heaven knows how it ever climbed two stories and got into my room. Through the door, through the furnace ducts, or through the water pipes? With its sharp rustling and with its scurrying feet, it was inescapably there as soon as I turned off the light. Now and then I heard it plopping down from some higher place onto the stone floor. An unpleasant sound. I was weary and in despair. But the mouse would not be exorcized. It didn't stop its work for a minute. I turned the light on and off about thirty times that night to make its stay in my room disagreeable. I even got out of bed, tired as I was, and opened the door so that it might run out. But it was no use. The assiduous creature never even thought of being frightened away and giving up its struggle for existence so easily. Whenever I turned on the light an innocent, malicious quiet at once ensued. As soon as it was dark again, the busy, rustling sound immediately began anew; it was as though someone had upset a waste-paper basket and was rummaging around in it with the light, discreet, well-trained and twinkling fingers of a spy. Not until nearly two o'clock did it occur to me that on the night-table near my bed there were several menthol lozenges that I used to take to fight off my irrepressible craving for tobacco. I turned on the light, got up again and looked at the table. Of course! Some of the lozenges were missing. The busy mouse had dragged them away to feed its young. "So, it's a mouse-father," I thought, "a house-father!" I craftily hid the pungent candy in the drawer, hoping that the unmercifully busy rodent, not finding the sweet food, would transfer its battle for existence to some other place. Of course I was doomed to disappointment. The rustling in the dark grew even more active and quick, even sharper still, with sudden perplexity. It invaded my over-tired senses from all sides like the stacatto music of the most tenacious will to life. Sometimes it was very close to me, and sometimes it was at the other end of the room, on the bookcase. But again and again it returned to the night-table, almost frenzied with disappointment and aroused recollection. I had never heard anything that could adequately be compared with the relentlessness of that anxious, scurrying to and fro over and over again. No doubt it may sound comical, but I had a more than distinct impression of that mouse's peculiar, strong, and unique personality.

Finally I decided to accost the personality of that mouse, to catch it in the very act, to make it visible with a cunning ruse. Noiselessly and slowly I moved my hand towards the light-switch and quickly snapped it on. The surprise succeeded completely. The outwitted creature was standing upright at the table leg up which it was trying to climb for the hundredth time although the smoothness of the wood balked it time and again. But now the mouse slid to the ground and cowered in fright against the table leg, as though the leg could offer it protection. The mouse did not run away. Presumably its strength had deserted it at that moment after so many hours of exertion. I moved my head close to it, slowly and relentlessly. The hypnotized mouse didn't budge. It looked at me with its serious, alert and almost philosophical mouse-eyes. They were the eyes, more-over, of a creature that felt itself caught in the very act of some shady kind of business.

When such things are expressed, they very easily appear exaggerated. But it really was so, or became so, after a few seconds of staring at each other. From the startlingly intelligent eyes of that mouse the unity of all life and the inconceivable metaphysical poverty of all earthly creatures looked out at me. Human eyes never have that look, that depth, and that readiness to die. A dog's look, in spite of all its abysmal sadness, is still only a dog's look. A dog's sadness is real but at the same time it is also assumed so as to win the sympathy of man. But my mouse was a domestic animal only in a limited sense. It was rather a gray prowler that enters the house nocturnally from below only on urgent business. It made no pretense either to me or to itself. It knew all the cruelty of earth without the lying belief in any mercy. It expected from me nothing but what it might expect of a cat of magnified proportions: death! the end! The unity of all life and the poverty of all creatures stared at me out of those tiny prowler's eyes, full of a resolute intelligence that spoke to me clearly. I under-stood it. Every art of translation is difficult. But how difficult it is to translate the declaration of a mouse's look into human words, something like this:

"Well, you see that I'm done for, that I can't move my legs. What are you waiting for, monsieur? (This happened in France, so naturally, it would be a French mouse.) You've succeeded in striking the weak point in a mouse's nervous system by stealth, sudden light, and the slow approach of your gigantic face; and you have magnetically paralyzed my once so agile and vital power of decision. Your room, monsieur, was a splendid scene of action for me. So much paper to gnaw, even though its nutritive value isn't great and the writing on it often makes it poisonous. But then, those stunning bonbons! They deprived me of my very reason and seduced me into a grave carelessness. And here I am in an awful fix. Fortunately, I was able to carry off a little something for my family. It is Fall now and mankind is moving from the open, provident fields into houses, and with them, all of mousekind. It rains day and night. The sewer, which is our haunt, is flooded over. Living-space has been taken from us, and our perennial famine is breaking out. Only the most intrepid efficiency can then succeed in getting into a friendly room like yours, through impossible cracks, holes, and crannies. Suddenly I have all I need around me, and I find work again . . . Why a creature like me is alive I do not know. Presumably, you would know that better than I, with your gigantic head. I only know that my life, whatever it may be, means work. What could be more the essence of hard work than to find food or to procure food? According to my experience, life is nothing but the unremitting compulsion to find or procure food for oneself and one's family, which means work, work, work, to the last moment. Has your experience in the matter been different, monsieur? I believe it was work that has been my doom tonight. Well, what could you expect? The discovery was too overpowering. After weeks of privation, those bonbons! . . . Well, when are you going to strike the blow? Don't you see, monsieur, that I have completely resigned myself and am fearfully awaiting your *coup de grace?*"

No, this translation into human words of the look in a mouse's eyes is even worse than translations generally are. Yet, I flatter myself that any other translation of a mouse's look would be just as bad; for the unity of life and the poverty of creatures cannot be translated into speech. The mouse and I looked at each other for a while, gazed into each other's eyes, so different and yet so alike; and our alike, yet so different souls, touched each other in mutual, frightened astonishment.

Then I made a violent and distressed movement in order to release the mouse. It disappeared into nothingness like a flash. But as soon as I had again turned off the light, it resumed its anxious scampering to and fro, to and fro, with relentless tenacity, as if it wanted to show me that no philosophy is applicable to practical life. This time I surrendered to its powerful personality, but decided, as I was falling asleep, to get me a mouse-trap in the morning.

80

Oh! How grateful are my eyes for the joyousness of two little girls improvising a dance to the music of a radio! How my sense of living glows at the sight of a ball of blood-red yarn . . .

81

Why do people die so easily for an idea of power and mastery that means nothing to them? Why has no one yet died for some higher knowledge, or for a sonnet?

82

The time of man, the span of his life, is always a short reprieve from the gallows. Only children can swim and splash and be jubilant in the shallow rivulet of this reprieve as though it were a broad, deep, blue, mountain lake. Childhood's unqualified physiological feeling of immortality goes back to a still unknown act of grace performed by God, who thus reveals his particularly favoring love of the state of childhood, the same love expressed in the Lord's words, "Suffer little children to come unto me."

83

Artists use certain tricks of the trade to give their pictures *cachet,* and make them more presentable, no matter how good or bad the pictures are: varnish, glazing, glossy or matte finish, as the case may be; but above all, a fine frame that cuts the picture out of the bare reality of the wall and changes it into a window in which, so to speak, the sunny landscape of eternity is immutably fixed. What matter if the perspective is not quite right, and the shadows do not fall in quite the proper places upon this landscape? The frame conceals many an artistic infirmity without the onlooker's being aware of it.

History does exactly as artists do. It sets an entire era behind the frame of a name. It says, "Gothic," for example, or "Baroque," "Classic," or "Romantic," and by a magic stroke, the infirmities of a given era and its false perspectives become a stylization, that is, an *intent.* Accordingly, we too may hope that history will give our era a name and a frame that will politely interpret the exceedingly grave infirmities of our works as stylization and secret intent.

84

There are people who always want to be givers, and who never manage to be receivers. This inability to receive is perhaps the most offensive sort of human arrogance. Of course, giving is more blessed than receiving. For, by receiving, a person candidly and nobly admits that he is needy, weak, and a beggar . . .

85

Between talking and listening there is a relation similar to that between giving and receiving. Naturally, talking is more blessed than listening. What a self-satisfaction it is to babble when we have nothing to say. And no one remains more venomously silent nor listens with greater annoyance than a fool.

86

The true nobleman is less characterized by the way in which he receives honors than by the way in which he dispenses honors.

87

The journalist is an extrovert who knows everything that has been written even though he has read nothing. The literary highbrow is an introvert who knows nothing that has been written even though he has read everything.

88

Snobbery is a spiritual variant of parricide (by disavowal). At the same time, however, it is, like every expression of satanism, a spoiled and putrefied value, to wit, the perverted love-impulse toward something higher.

89

The interpretation of the universe *ex posteriori,* upon which all positivism is based, is one of the most successful promptings of the devil. Why? Because the devastating force of its argument consists of nothing but the simplest of all categories, the principle of identity: x equals x. For example, "A nation is the product of its geography."—"The individual is determined by his environment."—"The political aims of a group depend on its economic needs."—"The elephant has an elephant's hide because he needs it to break through the jungle without being injured."—etc. To the fool the teleological key opens every door, even the most secret one. By this terse, *ex posteriori* prompting, the devil succeeds in conjuring away the question about the great *a priori,* the question about the act of creation, about the *Proton Kinoun,* about God. Only the incessant realization of this question constitutes spirituality.

90

Only the sick man who no longer possesses it can estimate the overwhelming strength that is consumed by that senseless, interminable, mutual preening and posturing that is termed "social life." It is a concert simultaneously given to each other by the deaf, with earsplitting noise, the deaf who do not know they are deaf because each one can hear himself.

91

I imagine that a long illness means that God is rehearsing with us how to die. Like actors, we show up each day for rehearsal and, under the expert but relentless guidance of our director, we rehearse how to pant for breath, how to be weak of heart, and how to cough up blood, until we are absolutely sure of our lines, have overcome our stagefright, and are no longer afraid of the entire performance.

92

What a deep feeling of guilt when we say we have "given up hope" for a sick person. It is as though we had suddenly decided no longer to answer a friend's letters imploring our aid, or worse yet, not to listen any longer to a drowning man's cries for help. To give up hope for a sick man is like killing him before he dies.

93

The mystical trial which man must undergo at the instant of death consists of a humanly quite inconceivable loneliness and forsakenness through which his soul must walk, probably so that it will be supernaturally fortified.

94

'Except ye become as little children . . ." We are most like them in the dead of night before falling asleep, when we are furthest removed from our professional and utilitarian life. Everyone who can should use that interval to nestle gratefully within that feeling of security and surrender which is God.

95

God is too great for human speech to be able to prove his existence. His chief quality, infinite goodness, is demonstrated in His creatures by themselves, in that they would rather *exist* than *not exist,* despite terror, disease, suffering, and death.

96

The spring has two wishes to make it happy: that we drink of it, and that we look at it while drinking.

97

What we call daylight is only one nuance of cosmic darkness . . . Thus, inconceivable darkness, or better, the dense non-light in the space beyond all heavenly bodies, would be, in its widest sense, the primary color of this world.

98

Snobs despise sentimentality. To them, sentimentality means the chivalrous homage that the strong individual pays to his origin, all the more tenderly, the more obscure and humble it is.

99

True talent is recognized less in its amazing gifts than in its unselfish ability to admire warmly another's superior accomplishment. That is the *noblesse* of equality of rank. Though talent may be vain it will not let itself be blinded. Its painfully alert capacity for distinguishing degrees of value is the staff with which it climbs to greater heights. The hopeless dilettante, however, betrays himself by the unsuspecting impudence with which he is self-intoxicated, self-satisfied, and self-limited.

100

Whenever the conversation turns to miracles, the

majority of those present not only feel violent disbelief but a revulsion to the point of disgust at the thought that anything like a supernatural event could have transpired within assured reality. But the minority of the gathering feel the burning, yes, almost infatuated wish that something like a miracle, exceeding the limits of nature, might have transpired after all. Herein lies a basis for classifying human souls, a psychological trait that cannot be evaluated deeply enough. But one should not forget that both parties are prepared, each in the direction of its revulsion or secret hope, to risk a *fraus pia aut impia,* a respectively pious or impious fraud.

101

In the realm of the religious there are no compromises and half-measures. The most radical decision is the only possible one. One cannot—as so many good people would like to—try to adapt science to faith or the reverse. Mindful of the parting of the ways and of both goals, one must decide without reservation upon atheism or upon the faith of revelation. Everything in between is really quite groundless and, since it shies away from ultimate consequences, dishonest too. This "in between," to be sure, is precisely the area in which man lives today.

102

The geometric point where parallels intersect, where there are no opposites, where the fool is converted and the scoundrel reformed, does not lie in the infinite but in the poetic comedy, in a form of play for which we have lost the culture.

103

That force in man which is called spirit endeavors,

through all manner of influence, to prevent him from feeling at home on earth. Science does the opposite. Thus, in its superficial contradiction, science would be non-spirit in spiritual guise. But in reality, science too is an aid to the supernatural: Lucifer, the light-bringer, whose task it is, as an unwitting servant of God, to illuminate man's sojourn in the kingdom of paradox.

104

In many a science, as for example in modern psychology, the satanistic impulse can easily be disclosed. This type of science is generally only a tautological operation which replaces the usual expression for a known fact by sobering and devaluating foreign words. In a book on this kind of "psychology" I recently read instead of the simple word "feminine" the following preposterous verbiage: "the passively masochistic, fundamental attitude of normal femininity." The devil laughs . . .

105

The voices of most preachers and men of God on the various wavelengths of the radio, in spite of their thematic inversion, correspond exactly to the ordinary nihilism of the modern masses to whom they address themselves. By the very shadow which their voices cast, one knows that they can neither believe nor pray. But one thing they can do: they can bore God to extinction with their unctuous, advertising tone which is uncannily inerchangeable for Jesus or Listerine mouthwash.

106

Nationalism as a heretical religion is based on the

erroneous doctrine that nations have a soul and that this soul is more permanent, more "eternal," so to speak, than the soul of an individual. True religion, on the other hand, proclaims as a fundamental truth, that only the individual has a soul that can lay claim to eternity and immortality, but not some mechanical quantity or sum of individuals, whatever the venerable grounds of nature which may unite them. The sole exception is the mystical quantity or sum of individuals of the *Corpus Christi*. But this body is, in fact, purely individual. Nations, however, are individuals only within the false perspective of romanticism, and are permanent only as such. In reality, however, the same peasant family in some Alpine valley, for example, has belonged to twenty and more nations in the course of the millenia, nations that have come and gone; whereas that peasant family remained and continued to sow and reap its meager grain upon the same, stone-strewn field. Nations, yes, even languages, are, as this example conclusively demonstrates, only guises and costumes that man puts on and takes off again when their time is up.

107

Were I a chip I should do my best to fall far from the old block.

108

What is true in reality still remains a lie in a work of art.

109

Probability in a book is a presupposition of truth, but not truth itself.

110

The most objectionable words a man can speak in his creature-like fear of thinking and feeling are, "I'm too stupid for that," or "I haven't the head for that." Complacently remaining in debasement is baser than the debasement itself.

111

Spiritual dullness is a kind of guilt, even when it is a trait. For it is generally a defense mechanism and a distorted pretense of stupidity. The spiritually dull person is a shrewd fox who doesn't open his shutters in the morning in order not to incur the expense of an azure day.

112

The rare opposite of intentional debasement (spiritual dullness) is artificial exaltation. I knew a man who went to pieces by arrogating to himself a genuine state of psychological difficulties which were quite unwarranted, but which finally led him to the limits of humanity, where he perished.

113

Woe unto the man, skeptic or believer, who can no longer be spiritually moved. Anyone who has congealed into cold assurance is a prey to the devil or, worse yet, is a politician. In certain circumstances a despairing blasphemy can be holier than a religious service.

114

We always find a creditable explanation for our successes and failures, whereas other people, even those closest to us, generally interpret these successes and failures in a disparaging way. Self-deceit and envy are the foci of the social ellipses through which we constantly rush in our orbits.

115

His heart (in the sense of *caritas*) wasn't at all so good that his heart (in the sense of muscle) suddenly had to become so bad.

116

The most solacing religious principle that I know was spoken by one of the Fathers of the Talmudic *Mishna*: "Repent on the day before thy death." Perhaps I still have a good deal of time. And twenty-four hours of repentance are sufficient. Perhaps twelve hours are sufficient if death comes at night. Perhaps twelve minutes are sufficient . . . In Christ, of course, one second is sufficient.

117

Languages are not only the expression of those who speak them, but at the same time they are also the secret truth about those who speak them. They are the warrants that accompany the nations to the end of their history. A true philosophy of language would have to understand how to read these warrants. For example, in the romance languages "death" is feminine, in the Germanic languages it is masculine. Conversely, "love" is feminine in the Germanic languages but masculine in the romance languages. Between the romanic "love" (*l'amore*) and the romanic "death" (*la morte*) stands nothing but the eternal cross of the letter "t". The martial death (*der Tod*) of the Germanic peoples, on the other hand, is the neighbor of the deed (*die Tat*).

118

So-called critical and assumptionless scientific thinking possesses, in spite of all, the assumption of language. There is a nihilistic school which, for this reason, endeavors to replace the language of words with a mathematical language of symbols for purposes of scientific thinking. But what is the use? There is no escape from the circle of limitations by substituting one set of symbols for another. Language, i.e. expression by means of equivalents, is all there is. In this sense, metaphysics is no less exact than mathematics.

119

A major principle of historical-materialistic esthetics is, "Art should be one of the social weapons which change human reality." Let us examine this principle, or rather, this challenge, as to its content of truth: Reality, as a human phenomenon, will either be constantly in need of change, in which case, however, the demand for propagandistic art would be meaningless, since such art would only aid in substituting one unsatisfactory condition for another unsatisfactory condition, and so on, *ad infinitum;* or, if the marxist revolution should lead to the highest possible condition of social happiness (as it necessarily claims, like every revolutionary movement), then, of course, that major principle of historical-materialistic esthetics (the art that changes reality) is not only meaningless but a danger to the State, because it is directed against the attained condition of happiness; and the artist who is enthusiastic about change deserves the dungeon or the gallows (with both of which he has indeed become acquainted, as the course of the world in recent decades teaches us), if he had not chosen, as a sudden conservative, to kow-tow before the absolutized revolutionary happiness.

120

The inner lie of historical or dialectical materialism is shown not only in its relation to esthetic values but no less in its relation to psychology. The materialists do not, for example, reject the psychoanalytical theory of pansexualism because it is incorrect and can be proved incorrect, but because, to use their own words, it "leads to a petty-bourgeois, individualistic anarchism." What? The search for truth is not to be subject to the criticism of scientific logic but to the criticism of political consequences? In this way, historical materialism proves itself to be a conscious fraud, a scientific *Tartufferie*, behind which is concealed not a real striving for truth but a striving for power on the part of infamous schemers who wish to climb upon the shoulders of the oppressed in order to do the oppressing themselves.

121

Just as bad music is nothing else than organized emptiness of time, so materialistic thinking is nothing else than organized emptiness of the spirit.

122

For almost two hundred years the modern spirit has been horrified and indignant over the medieval Inquisition and the trials for witchcraft which it conducted.

Let me be clearly understood: nothing is further from my interest than to champion the cause of the Inquisition and witchcraft. My interest is rather concerned with the modern spirit's horror and most profound conviction that during the Era of Enlightenment it destroyed that demonocentric frame of mind by virtue of which both inquisitor and witch equally believed in incubi and succubi and, not least of all, in nocturnal conception caused by the devil. The modern spirit, that is, the naturalistic-nihilistic frame of thought, should not boast too freely that it could never lapse, or that it has not yet lapsed, into a situation similar to that of the inquisitor who believed that a witch had slept with the devil and of a witch who with complete subjective honesty confessed her unholy intercourse with the devil. No one can deny that both fascism and bolshevism, different in form but similar in essence, are two consequences of naturalistic nihilism, that is, of the modern spirit. And now what happens when a political sorcerer or a political witch is caught in the legal sausage-grinder of these two systems, of fascism or bolshevism? In order to explain what I mean by a suitable example, I shall resurrect from oblivion the case of Doctor Levin. The amiable, honest, Jewish Doctor Levin, Maxim Gorki's family physician, was one of those individuals, good-natured to the point of absurdity, who couldn't harm a fly. However, during the great anti-Trotski trials of 1936 in Moscow, this same good, honest Doctor Levin suddenly confessed that at the instigation of Yagoda, the GPU chief, he had slowly murdered his distinguished patient, Maxim Gorki, whom he loved and admired, by fiendishly administering a series of the wrong injections.

This sensitive and highly ethical physician who would not even murder a fly, and who at every moment of his professional activity was aware of the physician's Hippocratic Oath that he had taken, this Doctor Levin, before the presiding judge of the court, the state prosecutor, the jury and the entire Soviet Republic, made a complete confession that he had caused the death of Russia's greatest man of letters by administering the wrong drugs during his visits to the patient, day after day for several weeks, with premeditated cunning and at well-calculated intervals. Why? For no other reason than the order of Yagoda, the now deposed GPU chief, who in any event must be condemned.

May I most respectfully inquire of the modern spirit, in view of Doctor Levin's case, whether it still is so very certain of the progressiveness that has raised it far above the level of inquisitors and witches? The witch who confessed was a little guilty of having had unholy intercourse with the devil as the good Doctor Levin was of having murdered Maxim Gorki. Of course there is one difference, that indicates not progress but moral decline. Though the witch was innocent, neither she nor her inquisitor doubted the fact that the devil had a great weakness for intercourse with mortal women if they yielded to him. The absurdity that occurred thus occurred in good faith. In the Moscow trial, however, no one believed that that little, gentle, Jewish Doctor Levin cunningly did away with the writer Maxim Gorki, the pride of his country. The presiding judge didn't believe it, nor did the state prosecutor, nor did the stupidest juryman; and whoever pretended to believe it, did so because it was politically useful for him or because he was afraid. It is possible that the only one who believed the confession was the accused man himself (corresponding exactly to the hapless witch of yore), stupefied by totalitarian mental torture and perhaps by the drug scopolamin.

123

It is frequently difficult to avoid the suspicion that the highly extolled rationalism of the modern spirit is nothing but the rigidly painted clown's mask of a wild, unclean, mephitic emotionalism. Again and again "new sciences" arise that try, by means of their academic technical gibberish, to convince us that they are legitimate children of "pure" and "disinterested" reason, at least in their methodology. Some time ago, for example, a German military professor—or professorial militarist —invented a new science of this sort that answers to the name of "Geopolitics." The very formation of the word indicates that it is less concerned with theoretical research than with practical application.

The theory underlying this new science is of the most deadly self-evidence and simplicity, and I seriously doubt whether it was any more novel for Caius Julius Caesar than for us. Its basic principle can be expressed in a single sentence: The geographic configuration of a country, a confederation, a realm, with its sea-coasts, its mountain ranges and streams, its kinds, sources, and quantities of raw materials, its roads, railways, airports, its transportation system and traffic rhythm, its agrarian and industrial stage of development, its ethnic boundaries, its irridentism and homogeneity, its historical centers of gravity and cultural affinities and aversions—in short, the total, tellurically determined concatenation of forces immanent in this country or realm decrees its role in political strategy and strategic politics, the role which it is destined to play in order to maintain and, if possible, to raise its rank on the globe. (Attention is again directed to the curious compulsion to tautology, to the explanation of a phenomenon by means of itself, which *necessarily* underlies all deterministic and relativistic reasoning.)

We may grant that a sagacious examination of the geopolitical limitations of a country could furnish very valuable hints to the guides of its destinies and could quite plainly define the points to which these guides of the state might venture to advance in the great gamble of global competition for power. In the case of Germany, for whose benefit the Janus-headed professor-strategist invented the whole structure of geopolitical science, the latter should promptly have established the dogma that the German nation, by its geographical location, is hopelessly incrusted in the midst of the Eurasian continent, and that therefore, in spite of occasional, apparently favorable constellations, she must always become the object of encirclement. Nothing—the professor-strategist should have dinned into the ears of his nationalistic disciples—nothing on earth can ever free Germany from its geographic and historical fate of being forced again and again into the fatal situation of the *Besieged Fortress* in every war (and the more universal the war, the worse the plight). This situation may initially offer the advantage of the "Inner Line," characterized by inconsequential victories, but it must eventually lead to annihilation by the crushing superior power which the outer concentric ring brings to bear with the ever recurrent inevitability of natural law. Not even a victorious breakthrough to the Siberian coast of the Pacific Ocean could have changed in the slightest degree this tragic natural law which decrees that a warring Germany, no matter where she stands, must always occupy the Inner Line, that is, the line of defeat.

This hopeless "inland-situation" (excluded from the oceans) furnishes a key to the understanding of German character. Prussian-Teutonic militarism, with its manic-depressive sorties from the Besieged Fortress, is the psychological result of this interior situation. The hysterical cry of German nationalists for "a place in the sun," for "Lebensraum," and for "world domination by the master race" corresponds to the ancient Germanic claustrophobia which led to the migrations of the late Roman era.

To discover all these things, however, by means of scientific analysis is not so much our affair as the affair of geopolitics and of its founder, the distinguished professor-strategist. Intrepid as a soldier and incorruptible as a scholar, he should have enlightened the Bohemian corporal and Austrian barnstormer of Germanic hundred-percentism, his pupil and Führer. He should have explained to him that on this globe, shrunken by motorized speed, every German war, regardless of cheap initial victories, would inexorably lead to the destruction of Germany, since the geopolitical entelechy of the German realm decrees that Germany cannot encircle the world but must, instead, be encircled by the world. The sagacious general and dauntless professor should endlessly have dinned into his pupil and Führer the fact that, according to the principles of geopolitics, no people could afford with less impunity than the Germans to provoke the world by perverse barbarism, by paranoiac recidivism and by glorified gangsterism, and to arouse the hatred of long-pacified nations with the insolent stubbornness of immature instigators. He should, on the contrary, have incessantly preached to his pupil and Führer that Germany's only hope of occupying a worthy place among the nations lay in her renunciation of all dreams of expansion; that she should lock up the most dangerous nationalistic fanatics (including the aforesaid pupil and Führer) before it was too late; that she should devote herself with the greatest prudence, care, and pedagogical skill to the spiritual development of her younger generation, to a far greater degree than the commercial nations of the world can lavish upon their youth; and that this spiritual development should bear the character of universalism, of world friendship, of Christian mystic sympathies.

These are the things the founder of geopolitics would have preached had he been no strategist and no professor, and had his geopolitics been a genuine doctrine and not only a painted clown's mask of mephitic emotions. But not even the most disastrous and most complete defeat will ever make these emotions reasonable; on the contrary, it is possible that even more than in the past reason will become emotional. And out of the swamp of self-identification of armed nonentities with pompous illusions of grandeur there will probably rise into the next milennium the miasma of nationalistic heresy.

124

Perhaps it is a God-willed education through exile

that those who have irrevocably emigrated may possess a home only in the form of homesickness. All progress is a climactic succession of violent separations. The plant is immovably rooted in its little patch of soil, the animal roams about within a limited area, man leaves and returns. Exile, however, seen as a parable of the soul, is a state from which there is no return, for the guide-post upon which is written "Homeward" ever points only onward.

125

The dreamlike as a form of art, the avoidance of associations, the boldly incoherent, the tendency toward echolalia, the ladling about in an assonant porridge of words—all that, in its stubborn estrangement from the strict Logos, is the final artistic hideout of nihilism, often even with the pretext of having overcome nihilism.

126

I have experienced many varieties of arrogance, in myself and in others. But since I myself shared these varieties for a time in my youth, I must confess from personal experience that there is no more consuming, more insolent, more sneering, more diabolical arrogance than that of the artistic advance guard and radical intellectuals who are bursting with a vain mania to be deep and dark and subtle and to inflict pain. Amid the amused and indignant laughter of a few Philistines we were the insignificant stokers who preheated the hell in which mankind is now roasting.

127

The highest possible form of modern narrative writing

consists of the mystic basic facts of the spiritual realm (creation of the world, fall of man, incarnation, resurrection, etc.) depicted by the most artful and economical means of realism in the least spectacular events and figures of the everyday present. Only a very few of the higher intellects among the readers will recognize this symbolism but they must never lose the blissful feeling that the author hasn't the slightest inkling of the secrets hidden in his simple tale.

128

The matter of cynicism is often very complex. I recall, for example, that the venomously amiable journalist and critic S., many years ago made the following confession to me: "The other day I wrote a perfectly devastating review of F.'s book although I regard him as a pretty good author. Today I sincerely regret it. But I was convinced that F. was a genuinely and deeply moral person. Unfortunately I found out, too late, that he is only a dirty louse, like myself, for example. If I had known it in time I could have conscientiously written a very favorable review."

129

We humans are not only helpless day-flies that are unsuspectingly washed away by the cloudbursts of history. We are equally the tree-frogs of history, the barometers that predict the good and bad weather of further development. The paragraphs on these pages, for example, represent not only opposition to the prevailing spirit (along with many similar documents by others) but they are also a barometric indication that humanity will in the near future (be it twenty or two hundred years) radically revise its attitude toward theology and perhaps even toward theocracy.

130

Since man is only a short circuit between Above and Below, he succeeds in producing nothing better than the spark that burns out all the fuses, namely thought.